DARE TO RAISE
EXCEPTIONAL CHILDREN

Give Your Kids a Sense of Purpose,
a Sense of Adventure,
and a Sense of Humor

CLINT KELLY

ALBURY PUBLISHING
TULSA, OKLAHOMA

Dare to Raise Exceptional Children
Give Your Kids a Sense of Purpose, a Sense of Adventure, and a Sense of Humor
ISBN 1-57778-152-X
Copyright © 2001 by Clint Kelly
504 - 51 Street SW
Everett, Washington 98203

Excerpts from *How to Win Grins and Influence Little People*, copyright © 1996 by Clint Kelly, reprinted by permission of Wings Unlimited.

Represented by Cristine Bolley, Wings Unlimited
P. O. Box 691532, Tulsa, Oklahoma 74169-1532

Published by ALBURY PUBLISHING
P. O. Box 470406
Tulsa, Oklahoma 74147-0406

DEDICATION

For Steph, Shane, Amy, and Nate, with love. You've made our lives so much richer and brighter. May these memories remind us all again and again of what a rousing good time we've had.

CONTENTS

FOREWORD

"The changes I have seen," Ann Landers once wrote, "would twirl your turban."[1] She's spent more than forty years dispensing advice to the lonely, afflicted, and confused. Over the years her advice has shifted from bad breath to AIDS, from spoiled brats to gun-toting ten-year-olds. Despite the changes, Ann says the number-one issue people have questions about is families. "It's always been that way," she observes, "and I suspect it's always going to be that way."

I suspect she's right. And I also suspect that many of the questions you have about your family are going to be answered in this outstanding book by Clint Kelly.

As relatively new parents, my wife, Leslie, and I have become baby-book junkies. We read nearly anything we can find on how to become the parents we want to be. And we've discovered that some parenting books are about as valuable as a wooden nickel while others seem nearly priceless. The book you hold in your hands, without a doubt, falls into the latter category.

I have known Clint as a colleague and a friend for more than a decade. And over these years I have observed his parenting skills first-hand. I've talked with his kids and seen the impressive results of his fathering. I know he lives out his Christian values every day of the week. So when I learned that Clint had gathered his most helpful parenting insights into a book, I was eager to read it—and I must confess I had high expectations. *If this book is half as good as his parenting abilities,* I said to myself, *I know it will be worth my while.*

---

[1] Source unknown.

I wasn't disappointed. On the contrary, I believe *Dare to Raise Exceptional Children* will not only provide you with many of the answers you are seeking in the difficult task of parenting your children, but it will do so while making you laugh out loud. Clint is a master at weaving wit and wisdom together with his words. He is immensely practical, unusually entertaining, and thoroughly biblical.

Read this book for all it's worth. I don't know if it will twirl your turban, but it just might revolutionize your family.

Les Parrott III, Ph.D.
Center for Relationship Development
Seattle Pacific University

INTRODUCTION

Actor Martin Sheen describes "creative" frustration as the act of setting your hair on fire, then putting it out with a hammer. Sounds more like the definition of "parenthood" to me.

Several four-alarm blazes have raced through my hoary mane since October 4, 1973, when the doctor pronounced, "It's a girl!" (He knew I'd figure it out on my own, but why prolong the suspense?) In ensuing years, three more proclamations of "It's a boy!"; "It's a girl!"; and "It's a boy!", respectively, were made relative to my offspring. The numerous hammer dents in the paternal skull are forensic proof that children do take their toll.

Some future anthropologists should get a bang out of detecting the familial signs of wear and tear on this old cranium. "Ooh!" they will exclaim excitedly. "There's a particularly nasty whack just over the left ear." Wasn't that when a triumphant Shane, just sixteen, decided to beat the semi to the light upon exiting the drivers' license bureau, trophy in hand? "And look at this beauty way in the back here. A regular crater!" as a result of fourteen-year-old Stephanie announcing she would go live with friends who understood her better and cared for her more. (Fortunately, she didn't follow through on her plans.) Nicks, gouges, and furrows aplenty, but no fatal blows. And do you know what? We parents leave marks on our kids' heads too.

Much is made today of the dysfunctional family; of parents and children at war; of the emotional, mental, and physical scar tissue piling up on the American psyche from divorce, abuse, societal pressures, and a deadening indifference to one another. Pretty bleak picture, isn't it? That's because it's completely distorted. God means us to be fully functional—and to learn how to be so within the womb of family. The only clear picture of family as it was intended to be is His. Psalm 68, especially verses 4-6, tell the righteous to sing the praises of the Almighty God who fathers the fatherless, defends the widows, and **sets the lonely in families.**

How sweet it is! God does not intend families to beat us down and make us negative and fearful. No! He designs them to be a refuge, a sanctuary, and a "safe house" where we can breathe easy, receive nourishment and instruction in wisdom, and from which we can launch out to conquer in the name of Jesus Christ the King!

Matthew Henry paints a beautiful picture from this Psalm of Father God the merciful, the compassionate, and the gracious who uses His all-sufficient power *for the relief of those in distress.*[1] He is the founder of families and the Creator of comfortable familial relationships in which people can lose their loneliness. He made Eve for Adam because **it is not good for the man to be alone** (Genesis 2:18).

But Psalm 68 speaks of an even fuller purpose for the family. It describes God's family in the sense of refugees who have been given a new homeland, a livelihood, and a hope. Home, biblically, is where we go to retreat, regroup, and replenish our ammunition for the fight out there. Tragically, in a number of homes the battle rages inside. They have become places of cursing, ridicule, and accusation, places where there is no refuge, no repose, and no "R and R."

Children from such homes feel wasted, unloved, and exceedingly lonely. Such youngsters are weary, wary, worn, and painfully unequipped to make a solitary life of meaning, let alone marry and propagate new homes where life abounds. They are the new refugees,

---

[1] Matthew Henry, *Matthew Henry's Commentary,* 6 vols., *PC Study Bible.* Version 2.1J CD-ROM (Seattle, WA: Biblesoft, 1993-1998).

casualties of the domestic wars that ravage the land. The good news is that our children do not have to become victims of "friendly fire." Peace can rule in our homes. In fact, we can become the best of friends with our kids.

Please don't misunderstand me. I do not mean to set myself up as some grand expert whose marriage and children are perfect. I'm just an ordinary husband and dad with an extraordinary Advocate who wants my home—and yours—to succeed for His glory. I can't say, "I know how you feel," if you're a single parent, if you've been divorced, or if you've suffered physical or sexual abuse. None of that has ever happened to me or to my children. Nor have any of us ever been strung out on drugs, pregnant out of wedlock, or suicidal. All I have to share with you is the flawed wholeness with which we have been blessed, in the hope that you may take away something of value, just as I know I could learn much from you and your experience.

I also have too many bills, too many credit cards, too little time, and not nearly enough discipline in my spiritual life to try to tell you how to run your life. Instead, consider me a friend who is eager to relate to you what has worked for him. I want to share the sweet tastes of heaven afforded me through my wife and children.

You'll have to excuse the warts. You may not agree with everything I say or have done. You may not be able (or want) to apply every hint in this book. At best we can hope for an exchange of creative frustrations and, I hope, creative *solutions* to some of the unnecessary agonies we put ourselves through.

Some might say that you don't even need this book; that the Bible is the only infallible rule of faith and practice, and that it contains everything you need to be a caring and commendable parent. I pretty well agree with that viewpoint, except that we all need to know that we do not struggle in a vacuum. There are other strugglers too, willing to come alongside and exchange tips on what works in the practical day-to-day. Consider this break from routine an opportunity to talk over coffee or to chat on the phone. If nothing else, use this book to prop open the window of your heart so your children can watch it beat and know that you're human and you're pulling for them.

Children, just like grown-ups, need to be reminded how much they are loved and why they are special. If the reminder comes with a creative flair, the impact often lasts a lifetime. These images can outweigh the fears in life and keep hope in sight.

I have included throughout this book just a few ideas of how to say, "I believe in you!" or "You are incredible!" in a whole new way. If you are a parent who has already learned the value of praising your unique child in tangible ways, these may add to your repertoire. If you are just finding out how life-changing and attitude-rearranging a little praise directed toward your child can be, remember: The right thing said at the right time can change your child's life and outlook forever. And don't just limit yourself to the ideas found in these pages. As you are reading you will begin to think of more specific ways to encourage your unique gift from God. Above all, have fun!

The six Kellys honestly like to hang around together. We laugh, touch, and cry plenty. We get attitudes. We're noisy, crabby, too busy, and too proud. We confide in one another about our dreams, our defeats, our mistakes, our friends, and our maturing sexuality. As surely as God does not alienate, irritate, dote on, or ignore His children, we have done all those things to each other. On the other hand, you may be hard put to find a fiercer loyalty to family than the Kellys possess. I guess maybe you could sum us up by saying that we are *passionate* about each other individually and collectively whether the topic is dates, grades, school, church, letters to the editor, the IQ of the dumb cat, or chocolate chip cookies. If you're a Kelly, you do *not* take a stand on anything.

In this day of cynicism, pessimism, and other "isms," it has become more and more of a challenge to raise children who are filled with self-confidence and have a positive outlook on life. We would all like to become better parents, and we know that part of bringing up children who are confident and determined is to fill them with the knowledge that God and their parents love them unconditionally.

One summer we were out camping on the Stilliguamish River. Nate, twelve, was beside himself at the dazzling crossfire of shooting stars streaking overhead. He was so enthralled, he wanted to jump up and streak with them—so to speak. "Dad, I can't wait!" he said, wriggling around like an eager puppy, "I want to be with God!"

If a kid's gonna have an attitude, *that's* the one you want him to have!

And that's why I wrote this book—to share what the Lord has been teaching me all these years in hopes that it will help all of us to better relate to, befriend, and preserve what Will and Ariel Durant have called "the nucleus of civilization"—the family.

Chapter 1

COMING TO YOUR THREE SENSES

Stephanie Erin, our oldest, is twenty-six at this writing. Ah, me. When she was four, we were having one of those never-to-be-repeated lazy golden days at a park in Fresno, California. She and her stair-step brother and sister (both lower steps) were gamboling happily across the verdant lawn beside the duck-dotted lake. Occasionally a child would shriek delightedly over a newfound treasure—a stick for sailing, an insect for flying, a feather for tickling.

I was sitting beneath a tree with a book, exploring treasure of my own, when my parental periscope detected Steph making a dreamy beeline toward me. I say dreamy because she kind of half stumbled, half floated along, eyes fixed wonderingly on an object encased in her grubby little hands.

Caterpillar, I thought. *Butterfly. A gossamer-winged thing*, corrected the writer part of me. *A nasty, rusty, tetanus-encrusted nail*, countered my practical, albeit cynical, father part.

Oh, the angelic face of the child as she drew near to share with me, and only me, the precious contents of her sweet fists! Heads together, we held our breath as the hands parted to reveal a ball of duck dung tenderly cradled within.

The delicious irony of that moment! She expecting praise; I expecting something praiseworthy. Life had dealt us both a lump of duck dirt. What to do?

"Let's see if it floats." I hoisted her to my shoulder, hoping against all reasonable hope she would not choose that moment to play pat-a-cake with my hair, and swooped down to the water's edge. It floated.

Yes, I spoke to her about "good" and "icky," and washed her hands. I said that for the most part, ducks are quite agreeable, but like all of us they must do their business from time to time and it is our job to walk around it, not take it home with us.

RECORD YOUR CHILD'S FUNNY SAYINGS AND WISE WORDS IN A SPECIAL BOOK. READ SELECTIONS AT SPECIAL GATHERINGS OR USE THEM TO LIVEN UP YOUR ANSWERING MACHINE MESSAGES.

Interestingly, at one time I was a grown-up research ranger whose job was to determine which animals ate tree seedlings, why, and how to stop them. I handled deer and rabbit droppings, analyzing their contents for clues as to what the creatures had eaten for breakfast, lunch, and dinner. Those examinations were for the development of repellents that help protect young trees. Had my mother yelled, "Nasty!" and slapped those droppings out of my hands, entire stands of timber might have been devoured, and your house might never have been built.

What I didn't do by the lake—that time—was squash Stephanie's curiosity or make her feel like an idiot, two things adults are very good at doing. It is in such simple and seemingly inconsequential incidents that the well-being and confidence of a child can rest. We do not have to sweat every detail, but we do need to learn to examine the cumulative effect of our responses. If God were to slap our hands for every dirty, tetanus-encrusted thing we ever picked up, we'd have bloody knuckles.

Save your horror for the really big stuff that comes along later.

I have tried to practice relaxed vigilance. If, as a child of God, I possess the peace that passes all understanding, then I can afford to let a little dung go by without a biting comment. But I have blown it, as we all do. I have made too many big deals over spilled glasses of milk, and I've overreacted to bedwetting. The key is to establish a pattern of patience that can withstand a parental lapse now and then. Children are much more forgiving than adults.

God takes a passionate interest in who we are and what we become without stifling us in any way. He wants us to take risks, to taste life, and to experience the incomparable riches of His grace. If we want whole kids, kids who relish each new day and crane their necks to see what's up ahead, then we must teach them to use their Three Senses: a sense of *humor,* a sense of *purpose,* and a sense of *adventure.*

I began to get the hang of my Three Senses the Thanksgiving when I was ten. My pride and joy was Sunkist, a brilliant orange German roller canary. It didn't get any better than Mama inside the kitchen, filling the turkey with her heavenly bread stuffing, and Sunkist in his cage out on the front porch belting out a canary aria as pure and clean as a high mountain spring.

GUIDE YOUR CHILDREN INTO PROJECTS, PROGRAMS, AND PRIORITIES THAT ARE RICH IN ALL THREE SENSES, AND YOU WILL DISCOVER THE ANTIDOTE TO APATHY AND REBELLION.

There was but a single crack in my Thanksgiving tableau. Larry Richards next door had a demon cat named Smugs. That feline furball craved the hunt, and the object of its sinister affections was Sunkist. Smugs' favorite bunker from which to spy out the land was the pink camellia bush between our houses. He'd lie hidden for the most part, just the tip of his nose and muzzle showing, his whisker radar scanning the airways for bird scent. I'd usually shoo him off, but this was Thanksgiving and I'd dropped my guard.

Two of Mama's greatest gifts were gentle good humor and an unflagging faith in God. Her philosophy was, "If He wants you triumphant, honey, triumphant you will be!" "Home is where you hang your heart," she'd say, or, "Earth's got no sorrow that heaven cannot heal." If she was in a particularly expansive mood, despite some childish crime just committed, she'd give a stern look and say, "There's no pot so crooked, God ain't got a lid to fit it!"

I ran into the kitchen and gave her a squeeze. The promise of juicy turkey drumsticks, hot cinnamon pumpkin pie, and sweet potatoes drizzled in brown sugar icing will do that to a guy.

Then it happened. A terrible crash from the front porch meant but one thing: Smugs had made his move. Mama and I raced to the porch in time to see Smugs' rump disappear under the camellia bush.

Birdseed lay scattered from one end of the porch to the other, and the door of the fallen cage yawned dreadfully wide. Tears welled up in my eyes. I knew for sure that daring cat had just swallowed the Pavarotti of birdsong.

It was Mama who spotted the still small form, lying on its back, out cold.

"I-I'm gonna kill that cat!" I swore, looking about for some instrument of death with which to make good the threat. While I plotted revenge, Mama knelt and ever so gently cupped her hands beneath Sunkist's inert body. She loved that bird as much as I did.

How could she stay so calm? Rather than curse the cat, Mama chose to cradle the canary.

Then she did the most amazing thing. She carried Sunkist to the kitchen, turned the oven on low, and took a brown paper lunch bag from a drawer. I watched in astonishment, my anxiety growing, as Mama placed the bird in the bag and the bag in the oven! I knew then that my mother had slipped from reality. Grief does that to people. The turkey sat uncooked on the counter while Mama baked the canary for Thanksgiving. What should I do?

"He's just in a bit of shock," Mama reassured me with a wink. "Shock victims need to be kept warm." *Right,* I thought. *I* was the one in shock.

The first chirp was barely audible, accompanied by a slight rustling of the bag. The second chirp came much stronger and had me jumping in delight. Resurrection!

"Bird's done!" Mama sang in her best Thanksgiving voice. "Come and get it!"

I peered into the bag to find Sunkist peering back. He ruffled his feathers indignantly. I laughed at the reproach in his eyes. As soon as we had restored him and his home, he let loose with a victory song that could have been heard in the next county. I danced Mama around the kitchen. She beamed and said, "Not a bad tune for a half-baked bird!"

Mama had exercised the Three Senses while I'd resorted to thoughts of further mayhem. She knew that canary's *purpose* was to sing glory songs to its Maker; she was *adventurous* enough to attempt to revive what I saw only as a lost cause; and she had the good *humor* to season the whole process with joy. Hadn't she said a dozen times,

"Where there's joy, there's life"? Psalm 66 had been underlined to extinction in her Bible, especially these verses:

> *Shout with joy to God, all the earth!*
> *Sing the glory of his name; make his praise glorious!*
> *Come and see what God has done, how awesome his works in man's behalf!*
> —Psalm 66:1-2,5

CURL UP WITH YOUR CHILD ON RAINY DAYS AND READ BIBLE STORIES TOGETHER.

If my response to the attempted canary massacre had prevailed, I would have missed entirely the awesome work of God. Those whose Three Senses are fully operational see what millions never see because the masses are too busy cursing cats and attempting to do God's job of judgment and justice.

One of the most brilliant statesmen of his day, King Solomon, said, **Any enterprise is built by wise planning, becomes strong through common sense, and profits wonderfully by keeping abreast of the facts** (Proverbs 24:3-4 TLB). Think of your children and their friendship with you as a chief enterprise you have been given. To pull it off and to make it last, you need a business plan.

That plan should include a vision statement for the family. What are we here to accomplish as a family? Too often we only pose the question: "What will each child be when they grow up?" They and we need to see that each of us has been given to our particular families in order to accomplish something beautiful *corporately* before each is equipped to go their separate way. Whatever significant challenge each of us is personally given, it becomes the family's challenge to do everything within its power to affirm and enable each individual to satisfactorily complete their special challenge. We all, in a very real sense, become stockholders in each other's achievement or defeat. When the individual enterprise pays dividends, all enjoy the spoils. When the individual enterprise suffers loss, all shoulder the liability. In later chapters, we will see further how this corporate approach to family reaps solidarity and lasting loyalty through thick and thin.

The Kelly family vision statement might well be summed up this way: "We have been given to each other in order to spur one another on to personal excellence. We will pray, encourage, cheer, and weep with one another until and *beyond* the point each is able to stand life's gale without falling. We will give love unconditionally, forgive without measure, comfort at a moment's notice, and believe a good report always. We will create a family life sorely missed when we are absent, one to be mirrored should any child of this family one day be favored with a home, spouse, and children of their own. We will seek and support ways in which each of us can express our faith in God to the world at large. We will, with God's help, make a difference."

All the great companies that last and make a good profit have a clear view of their own mandate and future. Ask the questions they've asked and answered: For what purpose have we formed a company (family)? What are the strategic directions for our company (family)? What do we want the company (family) to look like in five and ten years?

To carry out the plan and vision for our family and to hone our children's Three Senses, my wife and I piloted them into essentially five areas of emphasis: summer theater, sports, church, short-term overseas missions, and what we'll call community enrichment (wholesome activities, volunteerism). These are by no means the only options available, but we picked them based, in part, on each child's particular strengths and talents.

Before we explore each of the five areas individually, note that I chose the word "piloted" to describe how we urged the kids' involvement. "Guided" would imply more planned forethought than we actually supplied. More often than not we operated on intuition, "gut" hunches, and selection of involvements we ourselves would enjoy since the parental time commitment is considerable. In hindsight, I can clearly see how God knit it all together.

PROVIDE MUSIC, ART, AND SPORTS LESSONS IN AREAS OF YOUR CHILD'S INTEREST. SHOW THEM THAT WHAT IS IMPORTANT TO THEM IS IMPORTANT TO YOU.

"Piloted" suggests that parents have the credential for taking on the job of selecting activities for their young children without implying force. I am fascinated by the Columbia River bar pilots to whom the helms of gigantic ocean-going cargo vessels are surrendered at the entrance to the estuary. The captains of those ships, as expert as they are in traversing the great seas of the world, humbly recognize that they are no match for the natural complexities and hidden dangers at the mouth of the mighty Columbia.

As specialized as they are, the bar pilots themselves also recognize that they too are subject to the constantly shifting riverbed and bar conditions. Each is successful only as long as they carefully guide a ship, adjusting, feeling, and sensing their way along based on what they already know in combination with a constant flow of new and current data from instrumentation and crew observations.

Here are the five areas we emphasized in our kids' lives:

1. Summer Theater.

Shane has always had a deep love of singing from his earliest years. He was selected at the age of seven to become the youngest member of the Northwest Boychoir. My schedule as a freelance writer allowed me to make the sixty-mile round trip to Seattle and back twice a week for rehearsals. Often the other children would come along, and all developed an appreciation for good music, choreography, and staging.

It has long been known that the arts bring out the best in all of us. The magical stage combination of lights, makeup, costumes, publicity, music, memorization, and teamwork is truly exciting, inspiring, and invigorating. Engaging in those activities, plus taking direction, practicing discipline, meeting deadlines, giving and receiving constructive criticism, and sharing the sheer joy of performing a production you have helped breathe life into is an unforgettable experience. The result is an unbeatable, sensitive, character-building blend. No matter your strengths or talents, or your child's, the show has a place for all—if not on stage, then backstage; if not backstage, then in the ticket office, at the lighting or sound booth, or behind the refreshment stand or the promotional desk.

When I saw the notice for auditions of *Oliver!*, I innocently figured it would be a natural opportunity for my then ten-year-old, Shane. But by the time auditions finished, he had the lead, my two daughters were cast as workhouse kids, and my wife, Cheryll, and I were Mr. and Mrs. Sowerberry, the undertakers!

How glad I am that the director coerced us all (except too-young Nathan) to try out. It became a family affair in all the best ways. Each of us knew exactly what the others were going through. Our table conversation took on a new cohesiveness, we were all headed in the same direction and for literally the same destination, and our pride in the finished product was all the sweeter for having accomplished it as a family team. Today, our vivid memories of *Oliver!* are mutually shared and relished. Six-year-old Nathan, far from being left out, attended many rehearsals with us and was at nearly every performance cheering us on and helping us with our lines, which he had memorized too!

TAKE YOUR CHILDREN TO LIVE THEATER, PUPPET SHOWS, AND SMALL ENSEMBLE CIRCUSES WHERE THEY CAN OBSERVE UP CLOSE.

When our family was featured in the *Seattle Times,* there was our photo, six years after the fact of *Oliver!* Although they limited the copy because of space constraints, it was unanimous that, under the heading **The family that plays together . . . ,** we noted this:

"We try to do things as a family," Clint says. "When the kids were younger, we tackled summer theater. Among the plays various ones of us appeared in (including *The Music Man* and *Working)* was *Oliver!* My wife and I were the undertakers; Shane had the lead. His greatest pleasures were the scenes he kicked me in the shins and pushed his mother into a coffin!"

Ah, memories!

Seattle Children's Theatre allows for a question-and-answer session with the actors following each performance. What a marvelous education. Once, my children were especially entranced by a marionette performance, and it took forever to get them to stop tying strings to their limbs and flopping one another about the house.

Don't make a federal case out of the evils of television. Lure them away from the boob tube with something infinitely more intriguing and engaging of all the human senses.

When he was a teenager, Shane won the part of Jesus Christ in his high school's production of *Godspell*. He had to imagine the Son of God in a whole different light. How did Jesus speak, move, and love at the Mount, by the sea, in the city square? How did He—could He—endure the agony of crucifixion? What did He see in men and women worth saving? Shane struggled with accepting the part at all and told me on several occasions that he didn't feel much like Jesus. Shane, as wonderful, talented, compassionate, and loving as he was, felt he could not measure up to the Messiah. What adult feels any differently?

2. Sports.

A dollar, please, for every torrential downpour we have stood in to watch mud-covered children kick slick soccer balls willy-nilly across a patch of abused earth. We have been there for baseball, basketball, wrestling, pole vaulting, and cross country. Our boys are built like swimmers, yet insist on pursuing several ghastly forms of running. Our daughters complain of having "thunder thighs," yet storm into competitive confrontations where Marine commandos fear to tread. Just one fractured tibia to report.

No football, thank the Lord. I fully believe that if someone were to organize a national bungee jumping team, my children would enlist. The only sport I joined them in was weight lifting—boys only. More about that later. It is good that they have things they can excel at where Mom and Dad man the water bottles and "spectate." The family fabric is all the more tightly woven because we are there for each other. We cheer, we pound backs, and we experience solidarity.

The bottom line on competitive sports is that few things in life run the self-importance out of us faster than a good knock-down-drag-out on a level playing field. Humility, agreeability, stamina, laughter, and tears don't come much faster from many other sources.

We need the sharp edges and flinty parts of us knocked off by something. Unless you enjoy cutting yourself on the raggedy parts of your child's character, let sports do it for you!

Be there to practice batting, throwing, or footwork. Make it to the majority of their games whatever it might cost you. Supply the occasional refreshments, cheer loud and long—but not too much of either—and say yes once in a while to support chores. My wife operated the Little League scoreboard one game and discovered that it was kind of fun. So glad were the coaches that she knew which switch to throw—and when—that the next year she was placed in charge of candy sales. A house full of chocolate crisp is no picnic, but again the family pitched in to sort, stack, and sell product until we eventually unearthed the couch and rediscovered what a merry band we were.

When Cheryll was vice-president of the league one year I determined to move to the garage, at least until the World Series was over!

3. Church.

If children early on can taste the good life of an active church family that is warm, fun, forgiving, and supportive, and where individual commitment to God is the norm, just look at the benefits:

- Regular, sound biblical teaching reinforces and expands the values you've taught at home (third-party endorsement); also, other dynamic Christians modeling their faith give powerful assent to what you've been saying and showing.

SPORTS ARE A

CHISEL THAT KEEP

SHORT THE WALLS

THAT TEND TO

RISE BETWEEN

PARENT AND

CHILD AS

ADOLESCENCE

COMES AND GOES.

- Prayers of believers work in agreement with you for your own children. Teachers, pastors, lay persons, regular Bible study groups, and youth organizations will covenant with you to pray and counsel your kids safely through dangerous waters.

- Service opportunities come through Christian youth organizations' leadership. Our kids were local and state officers in Christian Endeavor, a nondenominational society for junior and senior high youth that stresses teens taking leadership in the church through service. Twice a year they were given charge over an entire worship service with the pastor as guide.

- Opportunities abound for expressing faith. Choir, special music, drama, and personal testimony in front of the church strengthened our kids, and more and more they seized opportunities to vocalize and demonstrate their faith outside the church.

- It provides proof that the Christian life is refreshing and restorative, not at all dull and stifling. We've done whitewater rafting, jet skiing, watermelon football, and meals galore with the church family. For many years, the Kelly clan's favorite way to spend New Year's Eve is with our friends at church—with games, skits, mind benders, movies, and laughs by the barrelful. Never mind Pin the Tail on the Donkey—you should try Pin the Tie on the Pastor invented by daughter Amy! Everything's the same as the traditional game, except you draw a likeness of your pastor for the wall and provide a variety of wild paper ties for contestants to pin as close to the right spot as possible. There's something about a paisley necktie dangling from a beloved clergyman's right earlobe that will have everyone in good spirits in no time! Then, at fifteen minutes to midnight, it's prayer and praise with all participating, and when the clock strikes twelve, it's thank the Lord, light the sparklers, and hugs all around.

Our kids have never complained about going to church. All are members and have a vote at the annual congregational meeting. They know the value of being "fitly joined" with the rest of the church body both in terms of what they can contribute to worship and body life, and in what they gain from the other members, without whose gifts and talents they would suffer a spiritual limp. (See Ephesians 4:16.)

4. Short-term Missions Trips.

There's a sign on the front door of a church up the road. You can't read it from the street because the letters are modest in size, but up close they read, "Servants' Entrance."

Gigantic obstacles to friendship in the family are ego, pride, and "me first" attitudes. If the only things your family members feed on are television, films, magazines, and lifestyles of the rich and overindulgent, then you are guaranteed a houseful of "me's." What is needed are servants on a mission for the Master.

> HELP YOUR CHILD SOLVE A DIFFICULT PROBLEM—DON'T SOLVE IT FOR THEM.

Pulling the television plug, seizing the Nintendo, banning all movies and magazines, and chaining the children in the garage until "this generation too shall pass" is *not* going to build slime-proof kids nor tender-hearted ones. What they need—what we all need—is *challenge* with a capital C, a challenge so adventurous, so selfless, so purposeful, and so audacious that the mere idea makes us laugh and cry at the same time. God's expectations of us are that grand; His plan for us that stunning.

Challenge. The explorers had it, the pioneers had it, and all the great inventors and discoverers had it.

Sadly, what we all too often settle for today is a character-crippling mediocrity.

I believe we began to seek challenge in earnest around the time we were engaged in the Discount Department Store Skirmish with our first teen. She would not be seen dead or alive, tranquilized or stuffed, anywhere near a Blue Light Special. It's not that she was an intentionally snobbish girl, but she was newly thirteen and still a little unsure of which peer parameters she could tolerate and which she would defy. There was some unspoken code that said you did not work in certain fast food restaurants, ride in certain kinds of automobiles, or frequent certain clothing stores. Be seen in any one of these horrid places, and you could kiss your developing reputation good-bye.

When she was fourteen, I saw the brochure for Teen Missions International. For twenty years they had been sending teenagers around the world to Africa, South America, and the far regions beyond. Making concrete blocks and tying steel, erecting orphanages and mission stations, was hard work. They called it "Getting Dirty for God," and those who went raised their own funds just like real faith missionaries. Best of all, boot camp training—two weeks in a Florida swamp—would soon have her begging for a Blue Light Special.

I gave the Teen Missions materials to Steph, whose heart was already tender toward children of poverty and suffering. She read the materials, prayed, and announced that she would go to Brazil to build a mobile film unit. It would one day travel throughout the remote villages of the Amazon showing Christian films to villagers hungry for a Savior.

"God wants me to do more with my summer than just lie in the sun and go camping," she said.

Since the summer Steph went to the Amazon jungle, our children have been to Belize, Egypt, Honduras, and the Yucatan. Steph did another nine-month missions internship in Mexico City. Nate, who had to reach our requisite age of fifteen before hitting the missions trail, went to Venezuela to play baseball with a team from Christian Outreach International. No force, no guilt trips. Once the others saw the profound change in Steph and the deep appreciation and respect she discovered for all people, they wanted it for themselves.

The results were nothing short of spectacular. One Sunday night, Shane, fresh back from six weeks in an orphanage in Egypt, gave the sermon for Christian Endeavor Youth Sunday. If you could have heard and seen the conviction with which that sixteen-year-old exhorted the congregation to spend time with God and allow Him to shape and mold them as He was doing with Shane, you would have marveled. Our son continued to bust dishes, overcommit, say brash things, and fall behind in his homework, but heaven's fire lit his eyes! There was a deep, abiding desire in his soul to live a life of service unto the Lord.

It means you will have to risk much. Teen Missions is a solid, respectable organization whose staff have literally sent thousands of young people to remote regions. Their safety record is clean, and their ability to move kids and tons of supplies would be the envy of any military commander. But the *Amazon jungle?* Heat, alligators, and insects the size of a terrier? Steph's second letter, by very slow boat, casually mentioned the boys chopping up a twenty-foot anaconda that had threatened the local lumber mill. Have a nice day!

Yes, her mother and I were anxious, had second (and third) thoughts, and missed her terribly. But wasn't God a parent too, well able to sympathize with the total surrender of a beloved child? I asked Him to please still my nervous father's heart. I wondered what Cheryll must be feeling. Was the cost too high? We were lending our child to people and places we did not know and had never seen. Always the answer came back, **For God so loved the world, that he gave** [sent] **his only begotten Son** (John 3:16 KJV, addition mine).

We have gained infinitely more than we gave by sending our kids to the uttermost parts of the world. They have risen to the challenge, and what they have seen and experienced drained much of the adolescent surliness, defiance, and nastiness right out of them. I am seriously praying about taking the cure myself. More about these trips later.

> TEACH YOUR CHILDREN TO BE DEFINITE IN THEIR PRAYERS, TO NOT BE AFRAID TO TAKE A RISK WITH THEIR FAITH. IF YOU DO THE SAME, YOU WILL BE AN EXAMPLE WITH YOUR OWN LIFE.

5. Community enrichment.

There was the time I learned that my oldest son wished we had let him opt out of dance classes sooner than we did. We missed the signals, but he allows there were benefits.

We do not advocate busyness simply for the sake of occupying idle hands and bodies. Dance, besides teaching grace, balance, music, exercise, and discipline, provides opportunity for public exposure, presentation, and poise. For your child, these same skills might come from cheerleading or performing magic tricks for birthday parties.

As a restaurant manager, I interviewed dozens of young people who were fidgety, unkempt, bored, unlearned, cynical, and under-challenged. They were, I am sorry to say, more the norm than the exception. It is almost as if today's young people have been abandoned to their own devices, and we know all too well what devices they can develop.

My eldest daughter, on the other hand, had an extensive resume of volunteer activities and the self-confidence to go with them by the time she was fourteen. Before she graduated from high school, she had worked with children at an Easter Seals camp, with mentally retarded adults for Volunteers of America, at the local animal shelter caring for everything from geese to kittens, and on the youth advisory board of the local mall where she modeled for fashion shows. She was also interviewed on the radio and helped organize fund-raisers for charitable causes.

These kinds of involvement teach some very important lessons: 1) I do not have to be despised for my youth; 2) I can make a contribution; 3) Not everything I do requires that I be paid; 4) It is fun and rewarding to do something for others; 5) Being involved in building others up is more stimulating and fulfilling than "vegging" or creating mayhem; 6) I can begin at a young age preparing a portfolio of activity that will prove very useful when eventually seeking paying jobs, college entrance, and community church backing for personal projects (like short-term missions).

Our society is constantly tearing us apart, diverting our attention from one another, and enticing us to separate ourselves from the family. Volunteerism and community involvement give us much more in common with our children and provide us with many more opportunities to work together.

When a massive housing project was announced for the lovely wooded ravine adjacent to our home, our whole family rose up in arms and attended public hearings and neighborhood forums.

Nathan was just eleven when he gave a very impassioned speech before a room largely full of adults. He spoke of the mighty fir trees that would be lost, the animals that would be displaced, and the sunlit trails that would echo no more with his summer laughter. The project went ahead, but Nate learned a valuable lesson about speaking up and being heard.

He enjoyed greater success at our neighborhood meeting where he testified to nearly being run over more than once by speeding motorists on the main residential drive as he delivered newspapers. Others told of speeding autos crashing through their living rooms and plowing up their lawns. The city heard. Not long after, radar monitoring stop signs and speed bumps greatly reduced the risks on Beverly Lane.

> PROVE TO YOUR CHILDREN WHEN THEY ARE YOUNG THAT THEY HAVE MUCH TO GIVE AND MUCH TO LEARN. ENGAGE THEM IN SOMETHING THAT ALLOWS BOTH GIVING AND LEARNING TO OCCUR.

Once when Steph was in college, she spent a portion of the night helping homeless Seattle street kids find shelter and clothing. It was one of the first truly chilly nights of fall, and business at the Operation Nightwatch booth was brisk. Steph and a teammate reached out in love to drunks, runaways, druggies, and folks just plain down on their fortunes. Was she, at eighteen, on the cold, inhospitable streets at 1:00 A.M. on a school night because five and six years earlier at ages twelve and thirteen she had given her heart and soul to stray pets and lonely, frightened children in her spare time? I believe so.

Adventure. Purpose. Humor. These Three Senses, if well developed in your youngsters, will shine when they have transformed into young men and women. They will love you for it. They will welcome your company, your approval, and your friendship as they mature. In a card from our kids one Father's Day, Shane wrote these words:

Hey, Bud [his nickname for me], thank you for being there when I need you. My hopes and dreams could not be shared with anyone else but you . . . and a couple others! I wouldn't trade you in for the world! God gave us a magnificent treasure. Happy Dad's Day, Shane.

Magnificent treasure indeed!

Chapter 2

THE BATMOBILE AND OTHER PROPS

The Rendille people of northern Africa are desert nomads who travel in small groups across the sub-Sahara. They live in tiny igloo-style huts made of wild sisal mats and animal skins. These direct descendants of the Cushites of the Bible (Moses' wife was a Cushite) pick up and move every two months in search of grazing land for their flocks and herds.

Rendille gratitude is expressed in a most unusual way. Instead of speaking a simple "thank you," a Rendille will grab your hands and spit into them. The blessing of *barrambarri* is then pronounced, which is their word for "may God bless you—may God bear you up as you travel."

If they're really crazy about you, they will spit on your forehead.

If they completely accept you into their group, the Rendille leader will spit into your drink.

In essence, this is what our kids have been doing to us for years. I'm not talking about the obvious. Parents have been in intimate contact with their children's body fluids ever since Adam and Eve first changed the diapers of Cain and Abel. When was the last time you had a soft drink to yourself? There's always some kid begging a sip and salivating into your hard-earned refreshment.

No, I'm talking about the later years when sometimes all you seem to get for your troubles is moist hands or a drippy forehead. It's like entering some monstrous "Twilight Zone." The childlike phrase, "I love you, Mommy and Daddy," is replaced by a grunt, a diffident wave, and a rolling of the eyes. You feel destined by the producers of this weird program to wander zombie-like through a misty moor of adolescence, where every kind deed of yours is met by a whine, a sneer, or an argument.

Stop! Remember the Rendille. What we take for spit, they mean for welcome. Could it be that way with our children?

As parents, we took on the business of draining the swamp for our kids. We're bound to get dirty, bitten, and sore, but once that swamp is dry—or at least, only ankle deep—and our kids are safely on the other side, our wounds will heal and often the very ones administering the salve will be the little wretches themselves.

As my youngest so delicately puts it: "Parenting is the most dangerous occupation in the world next to substitute teaching."

Friends do more than grunt at one another and take each other's stuff without asking. They willingly spend time together and talk in depth about what each other is thinking and feeling. They pray, sing, and laugh together so when the inevitable spit does fly, it is seen for just what it is—another way of saying, "Thanks for being part of my life and for bearing with me. I don't know who else could put up with me right now. I don't even like me! Yet there you are, totally committed to seeing me safely through to the other side. I know I have a bad case of the uglies right now. Thank you for not leaving me."

And when it's you who's doing the spitting, your children, your friends, will be there for you too.

One night our son mistakenly put hand detergent in the automatic dishwasher. It had happened once before—same kid—and in the midst of mopping up the sudsy mess my wife and I shouted at him, "Don't do us any more favors!" Talk about sending out the wrong signals! The message was the exact opposite of what we have spent years cultivating in our children. But because we have cemented a deep friendship with that son, the next day we could talk about the incident, apologize, and even laugh together over what twenty-four hours before had been awkward and humorless. That moment of restoration again reminded us of our absolute commitment to each other and how much we enjoy one another when all is said and done.

Cementing a friendship like that with your children, one that is damage-resistant, means finding neutral, nonthreatening ways of establishing camaraderie, cooperation, and appreciation for one another's abilities. Among the wonderful results will be the glow of mutual accomplishment and the discovery of each family member's uniqueness.

SMOOCH 'EM.

When the kids were seven and under and I taught at a private boys' school, we took part in a twenty-four-hour running marathon. One hundred boys and staff of the school determined to set a world record for the most miles run by one team in one place at one time. We broke into four relay teams depending upon our fitness and speed. Mercifully, I was on the Purple Pavement Pounders (PPPs), a team of twenty-five with far more flash in the running attire than in their feet.

The brave one hundred set a world's record in excess of fifteen hundred miles. I turned in a resounding personal performance of eight miles. My seven-year-old daughter went for eleven or twelve miles, and even two-year-old Nate ran the last hundred feet to the finish line between two lines of cheering "teammates." No, their totals weren't officially counted, but their inclusion in a world record event built their confidence and gave them a little ownership in a title they actually helped achieve. How? By their presence and enthusiasm, the official participants were encouraged and delighted and momentarily diverted from the pain in their purple feet. We like to think the students and staff ran a little harder and enjoyed themselves a little more. I know I did because my "younguns" were giving it their all. Last I heard, the record still stands and is recognized by *Runner's World.*

One reason children feel less positive about themselves and school, have low expectations of themselves and others, and just plain take less interest in life is that adults often leave their imaginations and creativity to chance. No creative stimulation may mean zero participation in the charisma of life. A national college Professor of the Year in biology, Harvey Blankespoor, says students just don't dream much anymore. "In this age of technology," he says, "it is imperative that we teach our students more than facts and concepts. We need to encourage them to dream dreams, to be visionaries, and to be creative, whether it is in the sciences or in the arts."

Jesus said it another way. He indicated that He desires for His people to be salt and light. (See Matthew 5:13-14.) We can't bring savor to a society or light the way for those who falter without communicating a clear vision. One of the most exciting rewards of having a family is that children raised in a loving, God-honoring, stimulating household can actually be a remedy or antidote for society's ills. Some people are just glad their kids survive growing up at all. But how much more satisfying to raise kids who not only survive the war, but take an active role in bringing it to an end.

How do you raise kids who not only don't fall victim to the world's moral and spiritual pollution, but who help neutralize it? You make friends of them and lead them into positive, selfless, character-building adventures.

We chose amateur theater early in our children's lives as a catalyst for character-building adventures. It provides as close to a perfect vehicle for engaging all the senses of all family members as any we have found. Good musicals especially teach a toe-tapping enthusiasm for life that is hard to beat. They put a song in the heart and demonstrate that a positive, hope-filled outlook in the face of difficulties helps us to rise above our human infirmities and fallen nature.

> ENCOURAGE YOUR CHILD TO TRY OUT FOR THE SCHOOL PLAY, THEN GO TO EVERY SINGLE PERFORMANCE.

My first real brush with the stage, unless you count the time in sixth grade when I was a dog-eared paperback in our school's production of *Treat Books With Respect*, came in high school when our drama department produced *The Bat*. I headed up promotions and got the bright idea of my friend and me dressing as Batman and Robin and swooping through the halls trailing fliers advertising the play. Batman has nothing to do with *The Bat*, but why split hairs? The winged warrior had a popular television show at the time, and this was high school—things didn't have to make sense.

My mom dyed my dad's longjohns black and came up with a cape from her vast storehouse of costume items. My father fashioned a construction paper vampire bat for me to wear over my hand with my dog's squeak toy implanted in the head for audio special effects. I wore a black ski mask and put cardboard wings on my forest green, slant-back, '51 Chevy with the moon hubcaps. A green, six-cylinder Batmobile that got stuck in first gear? Laugh if you must, but it usually beat my friend's three-speed bike for quick getaways.

"B" day dawned most auspiciously and things went well for a while. We managed to do our little dance to the Batman theme on stage in the cafeteria *before* the food fight started. We even made it to three or four classrooms before things turned really nasty.

Timing is everything and our timing was off when we found ourselves in the crowded hall between classes. Someone had put a price on our heads and offered a reward to anyone who could unmask the Caped Crusader and reveal his true identity.

Understand that I am a performer, not a fighter. But something down deep inside of me insisted that I protect the honor and privacy of Bruce Wayne, alias Batman. So I ran. But Dad's long johns bunched up, and I was brought down by the hounds. My bat was crushed in the ensuing melee, but valiantly, I gripped the ski mask, determined that my scalp should go before my identity did.

"Unmask him! Unmask him!" chanted the crazed rabble. "Tear off the mask and let's see the impostor!" (They may not have said the last part, but it seems like something rabble would say.)

It soon became apparent that scalping is not a pleasant way to go when you are the scalpee. Was Batman's integrity worth my going bald? It was not.

I relaxed my grip and off came the mask. I don't know who the crowd expected under there, but judging by their disappointed expressions, it wasn't I. I wasn't overly thrilled by their appearance just then either. Gathering about me what remnants of dignity I could, I gave Robin a look that said, "And just what have you been doing all this time, Boy Wonder?" He shrugged apologetically, but I could tell that, like the others, he was none too happy with who turned up under the mask either!

The dynamic duo slunk out to the waiting Batmobile. A sorry remnant of the rabble followed at a disinterested distance. Just to prove what superheroes we really were, I planned to squeal away from the curb and make them realize in no uncertain terms that their chances of ever getting a ride in so great a winged vehicle were now nil to nothing.

I popped the clutch.

The Batmobile stuck in first gear.

Batman and Robin roared off at five miles an hour.

Attendance at the play was mediocre. What came to be known as The Batman and Robin Affair took a lot longer to die—and live down. Rather than sour me on dramatic pursuits, however, the incident whetted my appetite for the thespian life. All I needed was to refine my technique and find a more reliable straight man.

William Shakespeare was right: The play *is* the thing. Put on a good story and both players and audience have the time of their lives. Include your kids and they will stretch and grow right along with you. To quote a gleeful detective hot on the scent in one of the Sherlock Holmes adventures: "It was a right snotter of a case!" You'll relish your family's stage involvement—and deepening friendships—every bit as much.

Oliver!, Lionel Bart's Broadway adaptation of Dickens' classic novel, was the perfect place to begin. Set in Victorian England with ladies in white caps and long dresses, kids in vests and nightshirts, and men in top hats, it was both educational and more fun than a loose goose in a foxes' den.

Involving sixty adults and children, including thirty-three cast members, it was a lesson in orchestration and community spirit. Our public school district hired a California playwright and actor and

TELL EACH OTHER

YOUR "MOST

EMBARRASSING

MOMENTS" AND

MARK EACH

ONE WITH A

CHOCOLATE KISS.

according to the local newspaper, "managed to organize the cutest horde of orphans since *Annie.*" Three of the orphans were ours, including Shane as Oliver, and Amy and Steph as workhouse kids. My wife and I played the dour Sowerberrys, undertakers with a decidedly sickly pallor of our own (which took a good half-hour to cake on).

For five summer weeks we perspired, memorized, and coached one another on our lines, our delivery, and our songs. Shane and the girls got to be cute and heartrending, while the missus and I got to be sour and sinister (obviously working against type). "Mrs. Sowerberry is a real shrew," my wife told the reporter with what I think was shameless gusto. I can still hear her rending the night with a piercingly accusatory, "Henry! Hen-reeeeeee! Where are you?"

Our kids roared with delight over their parents' antics and we over theirs. We misted over every time poor, abandoned Shane would sing "Where is Love?" and held our collective breath when it came time for the balky fog machine to lend a London feel to the scene. We fought the heat, wrestled a runaway coffin on rollers, applied each other's makeup, and took our bows together. We pulled for one another and learned that the play's success hinged on each of us experiencing personal success. So at rehearsals and while listening to the director's remarks, we applauded every cast person's gains and carefully sought to correct any shortcomings. We took the play home, to work, and even to church where we put up posters and received support from our friends in faith.

We studied the set designers, the lighting technicians, the costumers, and makeup artists. We sang and danced in various promotions around town to build an audience. We learned to gauge audience reaction each night to gain a feel for what did and didn't work and adjusted accordingly. We became fast friends with a wonderfully diverse collection of artists and artisans.

Since then, various members of the family have played pretend instruments in *The Music Man*, delivered newspapers and barked orders in *Working*, performed street drama in Honduras and Mexico, played living mannequins in a mall, played the parts of toys in a toy store, and delivered fake pizza in a barbershop-quartet review. Whether on stage or in the audience, out front or behind the scenes, we've been there for each other every time, and the bond that builds is unbreakable.

One of the most powerful examples of how an emphasis on performance excellence early in our children's lives paid off is the run of *Godspell* at the high school. Shane played the part of Jesus. Nate stood in for him at the end when the script required Shane to leave the cross, resurrect, and return to the stage fully alive. The rest of the cast were all high school and church friends in various stages of personal belief and unbelief, playing the parts of disciples and acting out the parables of Jesus. I have heard many testimonies from kids and parents alike about how being in that play in a secular public school was a turning point in their lives. We gained at least two new members in our church as a result.

I know Shane and Nate were strengthened in their faith. Shane was especially challenged as some of his peers seemed to watch like hawks for flaws in his "Christlike" character. But he survived the scrutiny and the grueling performance schedule on top of his senior year studies, mostly because of God's grace and partly because of his previous experience in a lead role.

The production went on to the state thespian festival and received rave reviews and a standing ovation.

Lyricist Lorenz Hart of the famed team of Rodgers and Hart once penned these lines: "Maybe there's a place where people never laugh. Maybe there's a place where kids don't kid, [but] that will never happen in a place like this."[1] Kids who laugh easily and laugh a lot, who have an inner joy that bubbles swiftly to the surface, make for a more harmonious home life. And when the joke is shared *with* you (rather than being *on* you, as in so many television sitcoms), making friends of your kids is achieved far more quickly and naturally.

This togetherness, this pulling for one another and taking collective pride in the results, used to happen on the family farm or ranch. Now it can happen when the whole family is engaged in a play at school, at church, or through community theater. Call your local arts council or the school district and see how you can help. Remember, half of the crew for *Oliver!* were support staff and stagehands. You don't have to act. Everyone, whatever their job, has a key role to play—just like in a family.

Have you been spit at lately by someone you love very dearly? Try to remember the Rendilles and the unusual way they show their appreciation. It is often in the contradictions of life that the lasting truth is found. How can blessing and cursing issue from the same mouth, a mouth that you once nursed and kissed over the years? That happens because we are fallen. Go visit the fallen ones under your roof and give them a blessing. For did not they whom Jesus loved spit on Him?

Barrambarri! May God bear you up as you travel.

---

[1] Lyrics from "Jupiter Forbid," from the play, *By Jupiter*, (Unknown publisher, 1942).

Chapter 3

LET MY STEPHIE GO

Have you heard the story of the meteorologist and the minister who never missed a weekend game of golf? One weekend, just as they were beginning to tee off, a thunderstorm struck. Soaking wet, they retreated to the clubhouse for an hour. Still the rain came down. With no relief in sight, the minister turned to the meteorologist and said, "You would think that between the two of us, we could do something!"

Cheryll and I sometimes felt like that. When the storms of adolescence were crashing all about us, you'd think that two parents who had eighty years of life experience between them could get a quick grip on things.

You'd think.

But the forces at play in family dynamics are much more complex than that. We had six people in our family at that time. Each has a relationship with the other and various combinations with three, four, and five other family members. All told, there were fifteen separate sets of human interaction going on simultaneously! The intellectual and/or emotional interplay between, say, the oldest and the youngest was very different from that between the oldest and the next oldest. I saw a documentary on a family with sixteen children. That family would have 145 separate possible combinations of human interaction in the same house!

You can be as open and friendly as can be with your kids, but if just one of them chooses to side with another, your system of checks and balances develops a crack.

Breach of trust is considered one of the most serious transgressions in the Kelly house. For example, we felt very satisfied to know that we could leave thousands of dollars in Little League candy sales money *unattended* on the kitchen table and no one in the family would touch it. Contrast that with the United Arab Emirates, where fathers wear pagers when they leave home in order to monitor whether or not men are calling their daughters behind their backs. The Kellys could not live under that kind of suspicion.

WHEN YOU SEE YOUR CHILD, GREET THEM WITH A BIG SMILE AND SAY, "HI HANDSOME!" OR "HI BEAUTIFUL!" GIVE THEM A HUG AND ADD, "HOW DID I GET SUCH A FABULOUS KID?"

One child decided to begin taking the family van without permission and drive to a girlfriend's house after curfew. The young lady in question let him know in no uncertain terms that it was wrong and that she did not approve, but for him it was a matter of testing the limits of freedom.

At 1:30 A.M. one morning, he drove home from a freedom run to a convenience store and walked right into the waiting arms of his mother. She had been divinely awakened by a "hunch" that not everyone in the family was present and accounted for. In the ensuing discussion/remorse/forgiveness/restoration, it came out that one of his sisters knew of his clandestine runs. He had borrowed her bike before the van became the more daring vehicle of choice. She knew it was wrong but kept her lip zipped. Had she confronted him when she first learned of it and refused to aid and abet wrong behavior, we would have known and the web of deception would have been considerably reduced in size—a boyfriend/girlfriend relationship might have been saved, a month's grounding from vehicle usage avoided, and a lapse in parent/child trust prevented.

We prayed and hugged at the end of this "all-nighter" as we always do when one of us has flirted with moral and ethical infidelity. The offender expressed relief that he had been found out. "I could never be a rebel," he declared. "I know too much about the love of God." He is a prisoner of Christ with a conscience that is tender, one of the best defenses against sin.

But where does the highly developed "righteous radar" come from that will keep your kids from making wrong decisions? Part of it needs to come from one of the best friends your kids will ever have—you. Oddly enough, one of the best means of instilling it is to send them far from you. There's only so much of that that you can teach your children. You know how they sometimes seem to take the word of the mail carrier or the bus driver before they'll take yours.

SAY, "IT WOULDN'T SURPRISE ME IF YOU CLIMBED MT. EVEREST OR DISCOVERED THE CURE FOR CANCER. YOU AND GOD CAN ACCOMPLISH ANYTHING!"

We need to surround our kids with other Christian role models who will reinforce the principles we have taught. They need to see that worldwide, there is a consistency of Christian faith, a unifying bond of love and practice. They need to experience that Christianity is not just something their parents dreamed up to keep them in line. They need to understand that it is the excellent way of life, the way that leads to eternal life. They need to know that their parents are confident and believe enough in them that with God's help, they can succeed—whatever the challenge.

We owe our kids a challenge—something so big that it could not possibly be accomplished without God's help and the family's backing. Sadly, this push-button society produces a level of mediocrity that not many will ever rise above. Don't let your children—your friends—down by settling for mediocrity.

Nolan Bushnell, founder of Atari, Inc., puts a different spin on that which deadens creativity:

> I have found that innovative people have a passion for what they do. I don't know if this passion is innate or not, but it can be snuffed out in a person. Think about it: how much passion will Johnny exhibit if after every time he runs around the house and displays passion, he gets hit on the head and is told to 'Sit down'? You're right, not much. This is one of the things that makes being a parent such a challenge. I see characteristics in my kids that in an adult would be fantastic, and yet occasionally, they drive me nuts. Sometimes, I have to catch myself and stop and listen to them. If I just say no, they will probably lose the inventiveness and imagination they will need to be creative when they grow up.[1]

We took the pent-up energy, the restlessness of youth, the desire to be free that was in our Stephanie at age fifteen and put it on a plane bound first for Florida, then for the jungles of Brazil. Through some mighty tests of faith in God and in her friendship with us, she began to form a vision for life. Soon after her return, I wrote down my memories of that time:

---

[1] From the foreword to *A Whack on the Side of the Head: How to Unlock Your Mind for Innovation* by Roger van Oech, Ph.D. (New York, NY: Warner Books, Inc., 1983), p. xiii.

The evening of June 16, 1989, was hot and still in Norwalk, California. On my way past the motel television set, I absentmindedly flipped the channel to the network news.

The newscaster was in mid-sentence. " . . . passengers not belted in were literally flying through the air. Twenty-five people were taken to hospitals, including one with broken ribs. . . . "

Another air incident, I thought, only half listening. *Glad our plane arrived without mishap.* A friend and I were in the Ramada Inn just blocks from Biola University where our denomination was holding its annual conference. I'd been appointed to be a church delegate and was eagerly anticipating the excellent slate of speakers soon to take to the podium.

" . . . Delta Flight 102, which carried 282 passengers, entered an area of unexpected turbulence about 25,000 feet over Alabama," continued the report. "The plane was about 40 minutes from Atlanta when it suddenly dropped . . . children were screaming and a food cart in the aisle hit the ceiling. . . . "

PLACE YOUR HAND ON YOUR CHILD'S HEAD AND PRAY FOR THEM ALOUD BY NAME. SAY, "THANK YOU, GOD, FOR SUCH A WONDERFUL GIFT." THEN KISS YOUR GIFT ON THE HEAD.

I thought of my four children safe at home in Everett, Washington, with my wife, Cheryll. All except for the oldest. Stephanie was on her way to a Florida training camp for a Christian missions project in Brazil.

" . . . thought I was going to die," a shaken passenger was telling the television reporter. "I kept screaming, 'God, please be with us.'" You could hear the fright edging her voice.

Occasionally during the months of fundraising and preparation that followed Steph's decision, Cheryll and I wondered if we had done the right thing in saying yes. True, Teen Missions International specialized in Christian youth projects and had a solid twenty-year safety record, but what of the heat, the alligators, the Amazon jungle? She had to be inoculated against several dreadful-sounding diseases, and our only communication with her would be by very slow letter. And prayer—powerful, direct communication with the One who loved Steph more than we ever could.

" . . . never been so scared in all my life," continued the disheveled passenger of Flight 102. "The cabin attendants were crawling down the aisles saying they had to get back to their jump seats."

Poor woman, I thought, straightening my tie in front of the bathroom mirror. *Must have been a harrowing experience.*

Indeed it was. But I didn't know just how harrowing until later when I phoned home and heard my wife cry, "That was Steph's flight!"

We had knelt together as a family to pray for Steph's mission to Brazil. She and thirty other teens were to do some puppet evangelism and convert a vehicle into a mobile film unit for showing Christian films in the villages of the Amazon. We asked the Lord for protection and that nothing evil would keep her from completing that which God and dozens of prayer and financial supporters had purposed for her to do.

Our daughter had narrowly escaped death on a flight away from us and we were not there to comfort her. I desperately needed my wife's reassurance and she mine, but God had purposely separated the three of us by many hundreds of miles so that father, mother, and daughter must totally and individually rely on Him.

When faced with turning back and going home, or catching the connecting flight to Orlando, Florida, Steph swallowed hard and prayed for the strength to go on. "I knew right then," she told us later, "that if I didn't finish the flight and honor my commitment to God, I would always be a spiritual runaway."

Should we have flown to her side; insisted that she come home and forget this crazy notion of proclaiming the Gospel at age fifteen? My friend and I prayed earnestly together in that motel room. We affirmed the biblical truth that if we trust in the Lord, He will supply. Satan would have loved nothing better than to scare her off.

I thought of the perils that the apostle Paul endured when Satan tried to scare him off—shipwreck, beatings, imprisonment, boos, and catcalls from a disbelieving generation. How would the young of the Church ever stand up to the doubt and evil in others if they turned tail before the doubt and evil they themselves experienced?

I was so proud of my daughter for staying the course. She had left father and mother and the comforts of home to be true to Christ, just as Jesus had to leave His parents and home to be true to God the Father's mission to declare a New Covenant.

The letters came postmarked "Brazil," telling of black streams of army ants, tarantulas as big as a man's fist, and the mighty Amazon River at flood stage. Cheryll and I took deep breaths over those letters, asking God to soften their all too vivid images. He did exactly that with Steph's longer, more glowing tales of river people in dugout canoes hungry to hear of *Jesus Christos.*

The TV newscaster completed his report with, " . . . the pilot had told passengers at the beginning of the trip that it was his last flight after thirty-three years of commercial flying. When the plane finally landed in Atlanta, the pilot was said to be crying like a baby."

I wept that summer too. First, anxious tears for my little girl far from me. Then, tears of joy for my big girl so near to the heart of God. She was securely buckled into her seat and was not hurt when Flight 102 plunged from the sky (no one suffered serious injury). In his letter to Stephanie following the incident, Delta's chief executive officer, Ron W. Allen, wrote, "We deeply regret the unfortunate circumstances involving Flight 102 on June 16 . . . I am sorry for any anxiety you experienced."

But later that summer, in a letter written from the muggy interior of a tent outside Belem, Brazil, Stephanie herself put away all regrets by echoing the words of the psalmist: **The LORD delights in those who fear him, who put their hope in his unfailing love** (Psalm 147:11).

We have since learned that the Brazil film unit that Steph helped build has traveled to numerous villages. Hundreds of children and adults have watched the movies, and there have been many commitments to live for Jesus.

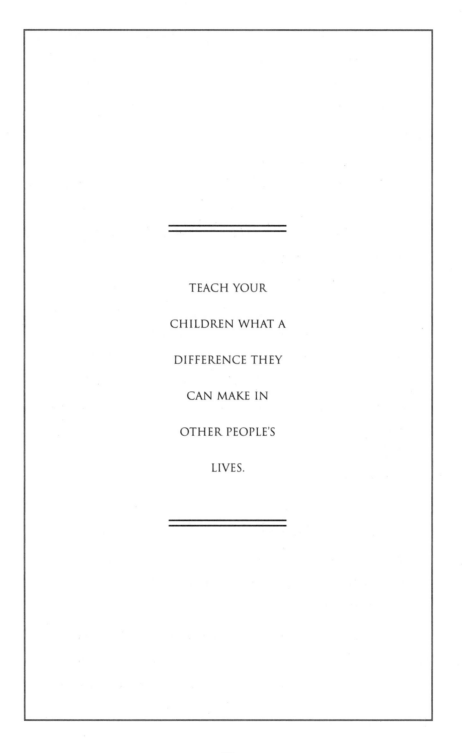

TEACH YOUR

CHILDREN WHAT A

DIFFERENCE THEY

CAN MAKE IN

OTHER PEOPLE'S

LIVES.

Part of the restless hunger in our children comes from a desire to do more, see more, and have a more significant role to play. On a short-term missions assignment, they learn independence, reliance upon God, compassion for the poor, appreciation for home and family, the importance of teamwork, insights into other cultures, and just plain how to share themselves and their strengths. They gain a new boldness when it comes to publicly proclaiming the truth, and they have fewer ties to material possessions.

We have a tradition of taking the kids right from the airport to Denny's for hot fudge brownie cake when they return from a missions trip. When Amy arrived from living with a Mayan family in Merida, Yucatan, and all the Kellys were happily parked in front of their chocolate delights, she calmly informed us that she had been stung by a scorpion.

EVERY TIME YOUR CHILD TELLS SOMEONE ABOUT JESUS, SAY, "MY, WHAT BEAUTIFUL FEET YOU HAVE!" **HOW BEAUTIFUL ON THE MOUNTAINS ARE THE FEET OF THOSE WHO BRING GOOD NEWS** (ISAIAH 52:7).

Every TV western I'd ever seen had painted scorpions as death-dealing scourges, but Amy brushed it off as a minor irritation in the line of duty!

Amy took a second trip to Mexico, to the poor of Tijuana. One of her excited phone calls home was about the opportunity she had to pray with a troubled Mexican woman. My daughter, my friend, spoke excitedly about the little children they befriended, the shiny black hair they'd braided, and the joyful Spanish church services they'd conducted. We didn't hear near as much about Disneyland on that return trip. Each of our missionary kids has had a major perspective overhaul. Expose them to the mission field and yours will too!

Missionary journeys will not necessarily make your child study harder, become less moody, or clear the table more often, but they will give that child a depth of understanding beyond their years. And your kids will thank you for helping them get there.

In *A Trail of Memories,* Louis L'Amour is quoted, "For land beyond the mountains is ever a dream and a challenge, and each generation needs that, that dream of some far-off place to go."[2] Don't tell your kids there are no more frontiers to explore. The greatest of all lies waiting—the frontier of the human heart.

When Shane graduated from high school, I gave him a prayer that sums up the paradox of strengthening close friendships with your children by sending them far away. You might want to send your kids off to school, to marriage, or to the mission field with this prayer:

DISTURB US, O LORD

Disturb us, O Lord, when we are too well pleased with ourselves; when our dreams have come true because we dreamed too little; when we have arrived in safety because we sailed close to the shore.

Disturb us, O Lord, when, with the abundance of things which we possess, we have lost our thirst for the water of life; when having fallen in love with time we have ceased to dream of eternity; and, in our efforts to build the new earth, have allowed our vision of the new heaven to grow dim.

Stir us, O Lord, to dream and dare more boldly, to venture on the wider seas where storms shall show Thy mastery and, where losing sight of land, we shall find the

---

[2] Angelique L'Amour, *A Trail of Memories* (New York, NY: Bantam Books, 1988), p. 218.

stars. In the name of Him, who has pushed back the horizons of our hopes and invited the brave to follow Him. Amen.[3]

The following are addresses of mission agencies with which our children have taken short-term assignments. We have been pleased with all three.

Teen Missions International, Inc.
885 East Hall Road
Merritt Island, FL 32953-8418
(407) 453-0350
e-mail: info@teenmissions.org

Teen Mania Ministries
P. O. Box 2000
Garden Valley, TX 75771
(800) 299-TEEN or (800) 329-FIRE
email: info@teenmania.org

I.D.E.A. Ministries
4595 Broadmoor Ave., S.E., Suite 237
Grand Rapids, MI 49512-5365
(616) 698-3080
ideamin@ideaministries.org

---

[3] "Disturb Us, O Lord" *The Bottom Line,* March/April 1992 (Orange, California Tech Serve International) n.p. Quoted from the Pilgrim Tract Society, Randleman, North Carolina.

Chapter 4

HOW TO BE CRAZY WITHOUT GOING THERE

Have you ever wandered off the beaten path? I'm not talking about having pancakes at midnight and meatloaf for breakfast. I'm talking major departure from the parental norm. I mean committing an act so spontaneous, so surprising—dare I say it?—so *shenanigan-like,* that at least one person wondered if you were a sixteen-ounce cup with an eight-ounce lid?

We parents spend such vast quantities of our time being responsible and accountable that we forget just how winsome—and powerful—the unexpected, the unpredictable, and the unannounced can be with our kids.

"Hey," you say, "nothing except the passage of time will ever make me interesting to my teenagers." I beg to differ. When we lighten up, our kids light up. Friendship is considerably easier with a parent who knows when it's okay to get rowdy. We must learn when to put the bullhorn down and pick up the trumpet. In fact, it's so important, it ranks right up there with learning "left" from "right."

TAKE A DAY OFF WORK AND "SPRING" YOUR CHILD FROM SCHOOL. GO FISHING. GO SKATING. GO!

And it'll make you doggoned interesting too.

One of my college professors, Ernie Davis, was interesting from the get-go. On the first day of class, he strode into the room and gave us an icy glare that froze the flame of mischief harder than four-day-old biscuits. A big wad of chewing tobacco stretched his lower lip taut as a bullfrog gathering air. He viciously planted a battered open briefcase next to the wastepaper basket and proceeded to carve an assignment into the blackboard with a slim nail of chalk.

Suddenly, without warning, Professor Davis whirled around and fired a wad of tobacco juice in the general vicinity of the wastebasket. The amber arc disappeared inside the ancient briefcase instead. His piercing eyes demanded to know just what we intended to do about it. Nothing, as it turned out. Our guffaws had turned to stone in our throats.

Ernie Davis came to be one of our kindest, most revered professors. But never, oh never, did we cross a man with such contempt for the symbols of academe. He was intensely interesting because he knew the stuff of which legends are made.

SEND A BOUQUET OF FLOWERS TO YOUR CHILD AT SCHOOL, "JUST BECAUSE."

When I became master of my own eighth- and ninth-grade classrooms at a private boys' boarding school, I was equally determined to keep my students just a touch off kilter. I loved nothing better on a drowsy spring day than to pace the rows between my pupils' desks and, in response to a particularly cogent answer, slam the palm of my hand hard flat against the desktop of a dozing neighbor. My hardy response both pleased the commendable pupil and rocked the socks of the dullard.

Upon another occasion, I asked to borrow a pen. Six ballpoints showed up at my desk within thirty seconds and I chose one. Then, without a word and in full view of my stunned charges, I snapped the pen in two and casually dropped the remains into the trash. For an unbelieving two minutes, the class watched me go about grading papers as unconcernedly as if I'd merely swatted a mosquito. Then, with the caution usually reserved for a deranged rogue elephant, the boy who had trustingly loaned me his pen raised a tentative hand. I called on him.

"Excuse me, sir, but you've broken my pen. Why, sir? It's the only one I had."

I continued to look unconcerned. "I broke it because I felt like it," I replied indifferently.

"But . . . but that's not fair!" he sputtered. The similar looks of outrage on the other boys' faces told of their utter agreement.

"That's your opinion," I said. "If those are the rules by which you choose to live, go ahead. I choose to live by a different set."

Eventually I lightened up, but not before we'd had a vigorous discussion about the standards of right and wrong. If man sets the standards, they are arbitrary. If God sets the standards, they are absolute. The breaking of the pen taught the lesson of fairness and its source far more convincingly and lastingly than if I had preached from my lofty station as an adult. The presentation of a brand-new pen to the offended lender didn't hurt either.

User-friendly parents also develop a flair for the dramatic, the humorous, and the different. My son tried to map the far boundaries of parenting once, and came up with these quips:

"Parents are like diapers for the training of life;

"Like suspenders to hold it all up when everything's about to fall;

"Like a kitten to comfort me in the darkness;

"Like a tugboat that keeps the big ship going and hardly gets any credit."

Anyone said to be as varied in their roles as diapers, suspenders, kittens, and tugboats has an enormous advantage in the crazy department.

It was one dark, stormy night in November, wild wind bending the big oaks and cedars around the house as easily as toy trees in a doll house landscape. The noise of the mighty rushing wind penetrated the walls of our home and made everyone thankful for their cozy sanctuary. Everyone, that is, except one.

SNUGGLE IN BED TOGETHER AS A FAMILY AND LISTEN TO AN OLD-TIME RADIO MYSTERY/COMEDY IN THE DARK.

Shane tipped his head toward the door. He looked at me with question marks for eyes. I knew that look. I was about to suffer. He was going to rip me from cozy to crazy, without so much as a blink. And I would go. My habit was to give a notion like this twenty-four hours to simmer and another forty-eight to gel. Here, within the span of fifteen seconds, I was to transform from stable, rational suburbanite to impulsive madman.

"Dad, wanna sleep out in the yard tonight?"

"It's 10:30 P.M., the wind is mach two, and I am a stable, rational suburbanite."

"Yeah, so?"

"Let's go."

You don't want to think too long about such things. Throw caution to the wind. What's the worst that can happen?

Forget I asked that.

The others mocked. Predictions of dire consequences rained like hail. My wife gave me one of those "you poor dear" looks but gamely noted that my life insurance was paid up.

Bowed beneath sleeping bags, a wad of plastic tarp (tents being for sissies), pillows, and flashlights, Shane and I plunged into the maelstrom. I threw down the tarp. In a beautifully executed flying tackle, Shane pinned it to the grass halfway down the yard. While he acted as a human anchor, I unfurled the bags. They took flight, I tripped on the "anchor," and the ill-fated operation tumbled into a writhing, giggling, sputtering heap.

It's Hurricane Edna, and we're making camp.

Snuggled at last in our sleeping bags a safe distance from the tree line, we watched in awe the clouds tearing past and the trees performing their frenzied dance. The moan and howl of the wind filled the void, and we had to shout our exclamations of wonder. We were surely the only two people on the face of the earth to witness the power and the glory of it all. Or so it felt. Though the home lights but thirty feet away beckoned warm and downy, we would not have traded our grand view for the sights of Europe—until 4:00 A.M. when the rains came. Then we beat it back into the house and collapsed weary, dry, and happy.

I like guerrilla camping. I do some of my best work when all the campsites are taken, the sun is setting, the gas gauge is near empty, and the car is loaded with four anxious kids and enough gear to bivouac the entire 101st Airborne Division.

On one particular occasion, we were caught at sundown on French Creek with not a campsite to be had. I looked at the kids, they looked at me, and I smiled benignly. They say the smile was

SIT OUTSIDE

UNDER A BLANKET

AT NIGHT, HUG,

AND MARVEL

AT THE HEAVENS

TOGETHER. SAY

TO YOUR CHILD,

"WONDERFUL AS IT

IS, IT WOULDN'T

BE COMPLETE

WITHOUT YOU!"

maniacal, but everyone knows you can't trust a kid's perspective too many years after the incident.

"All right, troops, over the side!"

They know that when I call them "troops," we are about to parachute into the jungle singing the theme song from an old Fred MacMurray movie: "Follow me, boys, follow me, boys. Pick 'em up and put 'em down and follow me, boys. . . . "

We formed a human—they say inhuman—chain down the hill to the stream. In the gathering gloom we hauled it all, slipping, sliding, and screeching to the water's edge. Because the only suitable beach for a campsite was on the opposite shore, we naturally ferried everything over a huge log handily provided for the purpose.

Only Nate fell in. I had assured him he could manage the box with the tent, and he had assured me he couldn't. He was right.

Later, beneath a star-studded sky, the creek chuckling beside us, camp burgers warm in our bellies, and the smell of medicated ointment wafting all about, we handed bandages all around and began a lively accounting of our blessings. Lo and behold, the very campsite that an hour before had been an accursed thing, now rated in the top three blessings right after "I'm glad I didn't break my arm when that boulder came loose," and "I'm thankful that branch caught me where it did instead of where it might have."

Now which campsite, of the many we've had, do you suppose the kids remember most vividly? Although, why they insist on calling the stream French Shriek instead of French Creek, I'll never know.

Our kids are our friends because between us, Cheryll and I have tried not to be overly proper, overly cautious, or overly predictable. When they were small, we bit faces out of their baloney. When they got a little older, we hired a struggling teen magician to spice up the birthday parties. One year, the boys and I found a clay bank on the Stilliguamish River that we slicked up and turned into a wilderness waterslide. We had one of the best times wallowing in the gray soup, painting ourselves head to toe in clay muck, and playing King of the Slippery Mountain. We laughed until we ached, and the only traces of humanity showing were our teeth and our eyes.

And don't tell anyone, but my wife and I are secret shoppers. We are hired by a national company to "shop" fast food restaurants, florists, department stores, car stereo outlets, and home improvement firms. We supply a "report card" on how we were treated, how the food tasted, or how the flowers looked. What we're paid hardly covers our time, but it's just wacky enough to keep us interested. Plus, it sets an example for the kids.

A LITTLE CREATIVE DARING-DO ON YOUR PART WILL DELIGHT YOUR CHILDREN AND HELP THEM VIEW YOU MORE AS AN ALLY THAN AN OVERSEER.

We've encouraged them to kayak for whales, model in fashion shows, go on the radio, write letters to the editor, march in anti-abortion demonstrations, and deep sea fish. We've told them early and often that they are mighty men and women of God.

They are not allowed to drive when my wife is in the car, however. Some adventures you simply can't rush. Hers is a considerably more practical view of daredeviltry than mine anyway, something along the lines of: "Even swashbucklers have to wash their swashes and polish their buckles once in a while."

I'll never forget the Great Toilet Paper Caper. It was a night when two of my least favorite things were occurring simultaneously—a female slumber party in our living room, and talk of TPing

So-and-So's house. I don't like slumber parties because it's usually my slumber that's disturbed. I don't like TPing because it is not a pleasant thing to wake up to on a drizzly morning. Put the two together and I will give fathering a serious review.

On the night in question, our living room looked like an emergency shelter for flood victims. Bedrolls, open bags of garish orange cheese puffs, slippers in the shapes of lambs and grizzly bears, and numerous hairdryers with enough combined electrical demand to black out half of Chicago were strewn throughout the room.

Slumber was the furthest thing from these girls' minds. Plots were hatching faster than mayflies on a summer's night. The Friday Night High School Football Game of the Entire Century had just been played, Bruins mixing it up with Seagulls in a zoological grudge match of cosmic proportions. I don't remember who won, but who cared? Jason Such-and-So had left the game early, and was he going to TP Linda Whozit's house in retaliation for the massive TP raid she pulled off with Carla What's-Her-Face the night of the Homecoming rally? If Jason Such-and-So left early, you can bet his best bud Chris With-the-Cute-Hair will be right in there stringing toilet paper from barbecue to bug zapper with a whole forest's worth of *Charmin Extra Soft*.

"So let's hit them before they hit us!" announced my daughter with all the sweetness of a good-natured cobra. "At least we can divert them, then we'll post a guard all night to make sure they don't strike back!"

She was declared Queen of Egypt on the spot and her adoring subjects offered sacks of cheese puffs in obeisance to her charms. I was wondering at how quickly the problem had gone from Linda Whozit's and Carla What's-Her-Face's to ours. Though our property didn't even adjoin theirs, we had given sanctuary to known TPers. We were now marked as prime targets of a TP spree.

Just then, Carla screamed so pitifully that I thought maybe her best hairdryer had died, but it was worse than that. The girls had no wheels. They were stranded on the most deserted of islands without a wheel to their names. Jason's house was a good three miles away, and no one's Lambchop slippers would make it that far.

Why the thought came to me, I don't know. I'd rather guess the time a tranquilizer will wear off a sedated pit bull than pile into a car with six screaming girls and half a railroad car of toilet paper. But that's exactly where I was a half-hour later.

"I can't believe you're doing this, Dad. Omigosh!" squealed Stephanie happily as we pulled away from Linda's house with a trunk full of toilet paper. Her parents store it by the case. I am convinced they are a family of professional TPers who smuggle contraband toilet paper through Colombia.

"Omigosh, Dad, omigosh!" The defrosters were no match for six breathy girls and my youngest son, Nate, who was convinced the ensuing Toilet Paper Duel would rival pro wrestling's Texas Death Match for sheer entertainment.

I was feeling a little giddy myself. I carefully and coolly maneuvered the getaway car down the back streets in search of Jason's place. Was TPing a felony? I wished I'd kissed my wife good-bye.

"There, Dad, there! Omigosh, stop the car! Isn't that it?" shouted daughter Amy. Carla and Linda verified that it was indeed the scene of the crime. I quickly doused the lights and slid the car to the curb.

Jason's house was ablaze with light and not a curtain drawn. Someone moved in the kitchen and Kathy Eye Shadow let out a startled cry that was instantly strangled by a mouthful of toilet paper. We eased slowly around the block.

"Grab your weapons!" I hissed. "As soon as you're away, I'll hide the car in the alley in the next block and watch for you. When I see you come running, I'll start up slow like. You hop in, and we're outta here before they know what hit them!"

My daughters stared at me for one incredulous moment.

"Omigosh!" said one.

"Omigosh!" agreed the other. And they were gone. In the meantime, I prayed no one in the surrounding houses had phoned the police about a suspicious car and driver lurking in the alley.

The battle was a rout. No sooner had they hopped the fence and done minimal decorating than Jason Such-and-So, and presumably Chris With-the-Cute-Hair, nailed them with outdoor floodlights. Nate was beaned with a roll of toilet paper he was certain had a rock in it, and every dog in two counties took up the alarm. The Kelly Strike Force turned tail and made a beeline for the car. I started the car forward, and they all piled in gasping, laughing, and trailing toilet paper. We roared off into the night breathless and snickering with glee, a middle-aged accomplice at the wheel.

> OCCASIONALLY DO THE UNEXPECTED. LET YOUR CHILD STAY UP PAST BEDTIME. PUT CUPCAKES AND A CANDY BAR IN THEIR LUNCH. SPEAK ONLY IN THEIR SECRET MADE-UP LANGUAGE.

They never got a make on me, but sometime in the wee hours of the morning, Jason and his commando team made their silent rounds and found our slumberers slumbering, including the sentry. We awoke in the morning to find our house, our yard, and our trees festooned in pinks, blues, and greens. I went to the carport and found that my car, probably still warm from its clandestine adventures, had been applesauced. The brand was Motts, and forever after that car has been jokingly referred to as the "Mottsmobile."

Was that any way for a full-grown father of four to act? One look at my kids' appreciative faces and I'd say yes.

Omigosh, yes!

Chapter 5

REACH OUT AND SMACK SOMEONE

I like the old English cure for bunions which reads: "Make a poultice of cow dung, fresh fallen, mix with whale oil, and place on bunions overnight."

Do you think it would work for kids?

I wonder if it might just take all the pain, the discomfort, and the awkwardness of growing up right out of them. If it would, I'd become a cow herder in an instant and plaster the kids from stem to stern with an extra-strength dose.

Should you find that your local market doesn't stock the proper ingredients for the English bunion cure, may I suggest the more powerful, more proven effective elixir of the parental touch?

In the standard ten digits found at the ends of our hands lie the awesome power to reassure, commend, correct, instruct, shape, and orchestrate lives in balance and in tune with God's intentions for the world He created. Like the conductor of a great choir or symphony, the sure, the tender, and the urgent movements of a parent's fingers can draw forth incredibly sweet and moving music. A conductor sometimes demands and at other times woos beautiful notes delivered in harmonious concert, but most of the time they simply collect the divine sounds already present and direct them into a fluid, melodious whole that makes wonderful sense to the soul.

A father's touch can liberate or destroy. Increasingly in today's society, a father's touch is tragically withheld or applied in vicious, abusive ways. Experts say American children today are fatter, more suicidal, more likely to be violated and murdered, and score lower on standardized tests than their counterparts at perhaps any other time in our nation's history. Unstable, broken, and fatherless homes are often a significant factor, but strong, loving kids have been produced by caring, heroic single parents. In my experience, the difference between success and failure with children can more often and more reliably be traced to the degree and manner of touch—or touchless-ness—they experience at home.

WHEN YOU COME HOME TIRED AFTER WORK, TAKE YOUR CHILD ON YOUR LAP AND SAY, "YOU ARE A BRIGHT SPOT IN MY DAY!"

By touch, I mean more than physical contact, although that is a critically impor-tant ingredient. Solid, lasting friendship with your family means touching them emotion-ally and spiritually, building them up with a look, a smile, or a word. Your body language, your phone conversations, and your hastily scribbled notes to one another can speak volumes about the quality of your friendships in the home. You know what it means when your kids roll their eyes at something you've said. Do you roll your eyes at them?

I once read a book about a single dad who took a 12,000-mile canoe trip from Canada to Brazil to get back in touch with his sons. He did not want the divorce and breakup of the home to consume either himself or his children, so he filled their lives with ten years of preparation for this trip. It was an incredible journey they took together; and while I don't fault him for doing it, I can't help but wonder how far out of touch this family had fallen that it would take an estimated twenty million paddle strokes to repair. But he also wanted to build his boys' sense of discipline and self-confidence—and his own. It was an audacious undertaking, and I am an advocate of audacious undertakings for building family solidarity.

Whether applied in the thousand little acts of an ordinary day or in canoeing halfway around the world, touch is critical to a healthy, whole human being. It is, in its purest sense, an act of the divine; and when done in love touch reflects the image of God. One of the works of art that stirs me most is that portion of the Sistine Chapel ceiling depicting two fingers nearly touching—the Creator's and the created's. When the kids were small, we did a little thing with them where, out of delight or appreciation for each other, either they or we would suddenly sing out, "Touch!" whereupon each would stop whatever else they were doing and touch index fingertips with the other.

One of the most precious moments a photographer friend of mine spends with his eighteen-month-old son is during bedtime prayers. They pray together in German, the language of their ancestors, the boy's little folded fists inside the father's big ones—a three-way touch between heavenly Father, earthly father, and tiny son.

In the Gospels, we are told that people brought their **babies to Jesus to have him touch them** (Luke 18:15), and that **he took the children in his arms, put his hands on them and blessed them** (Mark 10:16). At the Mount of Transfiguration, His face shining like the sun, Jesus touched His terrified disciples and said, "**Get up . . . Don't be afraid**" (Matthew 17:7). He merely could have spoken the words, but He touched them first to calm and encourage them. Again, when He appeared to them after His resurrection, Jesus comforted and reassured the frightened disciples with these wonderful words: "**It is I myself! Touch me and see**" (Luke 24:39).

Again and again we see leprosy, fever, and blindness vanishing at Jesus' touch. To be sure, our human, finite touch pales in comparison to His, but we too can quiet, affirm, comfort, and befriend with a touch, a squeeze, or a hug. Although I do it all too infrequently outside the home, I have been called a minister of hugs by a single mom I know who finds such courage and strength in those manly squeezings.

PUT YOUR ARM AROUND YOUR CHILD AND SAY, "I CAN'T IMAGINE WHAT LIFE WOULD BE LIKE WITHOUT YOU."

When my Stephanie, my firstborn, first latched onto my finger with her miniature, doll-like ones, I thought I'd touched the hand of God. When baby Nathan, riding high on my shoulders, patted my cheeks with glee, I grew six feet taller. When little Amy put her fingers in my mouth and gurgled delightedly at the wet, wiggly tongue she found there, I felt like weeping for sheer joy. And when teenaged Shane, the big old galoot, wrapped his arm lovingly around my neck for a father-son photo poster that hangs on my office wall, I knew that friendship doesn't get any better than that.

And yet, we did it all wrong, the missus and me. To hear the "experts" talk, we fouled out long ago. We stopped heating the baby bottles—poured it straight from the carton. (I never once squirted milk on my wrist to check the temperature.)

We propped their bottles at night.

We sometimes let them cry themselves to sleep.

We smacked bottoms when their willfulness exerted itself.

We made them wear bath towels when the cloth diapers ran out.

We threw them back and forth through the air to each other to hear their squeals of delight. (We have come to find out since then that we probably endangered their inner gyroscopes—somewhere in their inner ears, I think. We didn't even know they came with gyroscopes.)

If we did it all wrong, then how come they now have no cavities, sleep through the night, and experience little difficulty navigating their way to the refrigerator?

From "wet willies" in the ear to "noogies" on the noggin to wooden spoons applied to the seat of learning, we have communicated to our kids by touch that they matter, they are vitally important, they are loved, and they have a solid role to play in God's plan.

> ROCK YOUR CHILD AND SING. GIVE THEM A SQUEEZE AND SAY, "THANK YOU, LORD, FOR SUCH A FINE PACKAGE AS THIS!"

Don't let society rob you of family touch. It will if you let it. "Good touch, bad touch" training—as valuable and necessary as some components of it are—can make you and your kids paranoid to ever get close. The entire homosexual agenda has confused the issue of "appropriate touching" in the minds of many a well-intentioned father or son. When do fathers and children, especially fathers and sons, stop being physically affectionate toward one another and why? My thirteen- and seventeen-year-old guys sat on my lap from time to time or lounged against me on the couch to watch a video. It's a relaxed, comfortable, and reassuring feeling, whatever the age. And when the crunch times of crisis come, you will find you have built a reserve of goodwill, attachment, and even devotion that will lift you over the rough spots.

Moreover, encouraging affection among siblings brings much peace to the family. In the home our culture often perpetuates the myth that sibling warfare is the norm. Sure, our kids have their battle scars from familial uprisings, but they also have a deep respect and love for each other's contribution to the Kelly home. They kiss, they make up, and they speak highly of one another wherever they go. That's not only normal, it's far healthier than treating their brother or sister as if they have a terminal case of the cooties. And it has a positive effect in every other relationship they have when they leave home.

Of course, the Kelly males communicate a good deal of closeness through ruder means than the females would like. The delicate ladies of the house express great disdain at our sweaty weight-lifting sessions, grunt-filled wrestling matches, and highly auditory "belch-a-thons." When Shane returned from his missions trip to Belize and introduced us to the game of "bloody knuckles," the resident members of "the gentle sex" knew that the ultimate in male offensiveness had been attained.

Here was the perfect combination of pain and industrial-strength touch—tailor-made for the macho psyche. The rules are simplicity itself. You and your opponent make fists and touch knuckles. Whoever goes first attempts to strike the top of the other's clenched fists before he has time to jerk them back out of the way. If the aggressor succeeds in making contact, he is rewarded with consecutive turns until such time as he misses, and it is then his opponent's turn to strike back.

My wife thinks the boys and I have been out in the sun too long, so we are forced to play the game in secret. If only I didn't bruise so easily and my hands didn't swell up like clubs, we might get away with it.

And what's wrong with wrestling? It is a time-honored, highly civilized means of testing strength, endurance, and muscular development. Where is it more socially acceptable to expand one's repertoire of groans and snorts? As surely as the "measuring wall" in the kitchen records the family's vertical growth, father-and-son wrestle-mania tracks increase in weight and musculature. As long as I was still able to pick my seventeen-year-old, 170-pounder off the ground and flip him over my back without landing in the hernia ward, *I was the papa!* But my reflexes today as Boris the Bear are slower than they were twenty years ago when I was Whinny the Circus Pony. I remember when I first noticed my dad slowing down. Sorry to say, it was of great encouragement to me—like some generational torch was being passed. I was taking my rightful place in the male line and it felt mighty good. I'm ready for grandkids, though. Bring them on!

CUDDLE WITH YOUR KID. FALL ASLEEP TOGETHER ON THE COUCH. LET YOUR CHILD FEEL YOUR PHYSICAL SUPPORT, AFFECTION, AND PROTECTION.

That some of these contests of might and main take place in the living room is unfortunate, but you can't always schedule these things. You can buy a new coffee table, but missed opportunities to flatten your boys—and they you—may never come around again.

I believe the most mysterious of all maladies is the teen years. One minute your kids are clinging to you for dear life; the next minute you are so many pounds of protoplasm that are very much in their way. One minute, everything they speak or do says, "Touch me, I need you." The next minute, it's "Touch me, and I'll scream." Dr. Stephen Yarnall, a fellow of the American College of Cardiology, gives bewildered parents of teens the same advice he would to a sailor in a storm, "Do what you think is best, ride it out, and try not to make things worse than they are."[1]

I would add my mother's two bits: "Hang on for dear life, and keep your eyes fixed on the road ahead so you don't get carsick."

Yes, do think ahead. Keep in mind the saying, "Grandchildren are a reward for not killing your children." As time goes on, kids want to be kissed and touched less by their parents as part of the natural weaning process. My mother raised me to be emotional, sensitive, and demonstrative, and I've tried to raise my children to feel deeply and to take a passionate interest in others. That means they embrace others easily, which can sometimes be a drawback. I tend to take everything my kids say or do personally and never want them to change. At other times, they couldn't change fast enough to suit me.

I would like to have frozen and preserved Shane at age fifteen. It seemed as if he had the most wonderful combination of personality, character, compassion, and joy, and was as fun-loving and considerate as could be. We were the best of friends. We said so and put it in writing and loved to do things together. It seemed like the best of times, and people would remark about our closeness and obvious love for one another. We punched and played and laughed—a lot. It was a high-touch year. It was also temporary.

As Shane grew older, he became more eager to see what kind of stuff he was made of, independent of me. As his life became more complex, he became more private and introspective. He changed career goals and other interests faster than I could keep up. I loathe change, and he was a veritable blizzard of change.

---

[1] Source unknown.

I needed to learn that Shane wasn't always going to be by my side. God has a whole other set of plans and purposes for him apart from Dad. I needed to let go and give him room to explore what else the Lord had in store for his life. I think, too, God was giving me a little of my own medicine. How much time do I spend communicating with the Lord? Just how close do I stay to my heavenly Father? How must He feel when I go off on my own and He's not invited? I so often take Him for granted. King David's invitation to **taste and see that the LORD is good; blessed is the man who takes refuge in him** (Psalm 34:8) requires high-touch, hands-on involvement.

It's been said that when you see a turtle on a fence post, you know it didn't get there by itself. Behind every successful kid-turned-adult is a strong support team of friends both in and out of the family. If you are an adversary to your children, they are doubly handicapped. Not only do they lack the benefits of your friendship, they swim upstream against the stress of being at odds with you. Go to them now, bury the hatchet, and ask them to be your friends. Their security—and yours—depends upon it.

It is amazing that the pat of welcome, the punch of playfulness, the rod of discipline, the accepting squeeze of forgiveness, and the warm hug of love are to be administered by the same parental arm! I like the way lions manage it. The lioness greets her cubs and patiently endures their playful tussles. One minute she's taking them by the scruff of the neck and giving them a good shake or cuffing them stoutly with her paw to shape them up; the next minute her great pink towel of a tongue is giving them a good washing down. Discipline, maintenance, and care—all seemingly administered without malice or indifference. And lions are a tightly knit bunch.

We also show the depth of our commitment to one another by the words we use. On those days when you feel like parenting is too

ASK FOR YOUR

CHILD'S FORGIVE-

NESS. GIVE THEM A

KISS AND SAY,

"THANK YOU FOR

FORGIVING ALL

MY MISTAKES!"

much and you'd like to resign, you'd be better off not to open your mouth at all. Of course, I rarely take my own advice. Some of the most hurtful things I've ever said have come at these times of sourness. I've called my son a jerk, yelled at everyone to "Shut up!" (a phrase the children were never allowed to use in the home), and strafed the room with eyes ablaze.

If you fall into the habit of verbally brow-beating and belittling your child—and it is a habit—you will not only ruin a friendship, but you will give that youngster a distorted picture of God the Father.

Jesus used terms of endearment for His own. He called them "chicks," "little ones," and "My lambs." We tend to be more indelicate, perhaps, but our babes have been our "munchkins," "rug rats," and "little nu-nu's." Some days they are our "buddies" or "sweetums." They've heard me call my wife "honeybabes" and her call me "bug-a-dee" (don't ask). Lumped together like this, it all sounds a bit saccharine, but taken in context, pet names subtly communicate that home is where those special friends live for whom you would gladly sacrifice your life.

My mother loved words and used them judiciously to persuade newspaper editors, mayors, and corporations alike to see things her way. She used them on me with the greatest of ease, usually careful to select the ones that would encourage me the most. I was a great one for running in with a knot of snakes to show, and she was a great one for swallowing her dismay—and the word "yuck." She would say, "Oh, my!" with such savoir faire that I took it for admiring approval.

LET YOUR SMALL CHILD RIDE ON YOUR BACK, THEN ANNOUNCE IN YOUR BEST RINGMASTER VOICE, "AND NOW, LA-DEES AND GENTLEMEN, THE MOMENT YOU'VE ALL BEEN WAITING FOR! THE EXCITING, THE TALENTED, THE DAZZLING—JENNY SMITH!" THEN CLAP, YELL, AND WHISTLE LIKE THE ROAR OF A CROWD.

She also had a good deal of fun with words. Alliterations and a clever play on words were some of her favorite things. I played the grooves off of my 45-rpm recording of "MacNamara's Band," and every time they got to "Tennessee, Hennessey tootled the flute, and the music was something grand," she and I would chime in.

Every once in a while the words would come out of her mouth with, as my grandpa put it, "the shoes on the wrong feet." Her combination of embarrassment and delight at the results taught me the healing touch of humor. There was the favorite apology of this fine cook that some dish or other had turned out "tough as a dog." But one Sunday, in front of guests, she waxed eloquent and declared the fried chicken "dry as a dog's hind leg!"

The *pièce de résistance* in verbal chagrin was delivered one chilly day when I came home from school for lunch. My mother greeted me with an affectionate squeeze, a cup of hot chocolate, and a hardy greeting. She meant to say, "Hi, honey, take off your coat, and I'll heat up your soup." What she actually said was, "Hi, honey, take off your coat, and I'll hoot up your seat." Faces don't come any redder than hers did that day. That happened when I was ten. When I turned forty, she and I still exploded in helpless laughter over that one. All I had to do was look at her, arch my eyebrows, and mouth the word "soup."

Mother touched me with her original bedtime stories about Beetle Boy and Buzz Buzz, and old Fox and Owl stories I have told to my own delighted children. I can still smell the faint scent of *Emeraude* perfume about her as in my dreams she still takes me down the winding path to the "deep, dark woods" where the forest animals hold their "furry friend parades."

I shall never forget my mother six months before her death driving an electric cart around a giant supermarket like a stock car racer. She hadn't driven in twenty years, yet there she was at a frail seventy-nine cornering like a pro between canned peaches and flavored gelatin. She gave no quarter and expected none in return, and when she crossed the finish line at frozen dinners, I sent up a cheer. She looked at me as if I were a novice at these things, then smiled slyly. "Wanna go for a spin, Bub?" she asked. I thought instantly of the day the forest critters had held a race of their own and how wise old Grandma Owl had made the rest of the field eat her dust. Touché!

SHOW FAVOR WHENEVER POSSIBLE BY AFFIRMING A CHILD'S SECURE AND IMPORTANT FAMILY POSITION WITH WORDS OF PRAISE AND ENCOURAGEMENT. REINFORCE IT WITH A HUG, AND YOU'VE IMPARTED A GIFT WITHOUT MEASURE.

These are the kind of memories that will remain with your children long after you are gone.

On his website, Mark Dillon, a D. A. R. E. officer, suggests one hundred ways to praise a child.

WOW

NEAT

GOOD

GREAT

BRAVO

SUPER

A+ JOB

AWESOME

RADICAL

TERRIFIC

PERFECT
HOW NICE
DYNAMITE
GOOD JOB
GOOD STUFF
YOU CARE
MARVELOUS
HOW SMART
FANTASTIC
SUPERSTAR
EXCELLENT
WELL DONE
WAY TO GO
BEAUTIFUL
HOT STUFF
NICE WORK
SUPER JOB
PHENOMENAL
SUPER WORK
YOU BELONG
I LIKE YOU
THAT'S HOT
MAGNIFICENT
OUTSTANDING
I TRUST YOU
SPECTACULAR
GOOD FOR YOU
LOOKING GOOD
YOU'RE ON IT
TRY YOUR BEST

I RESPECT YOU
FANTASTIC JOB
YOU'RE UNIQUE
GOOD THINKING
CREATIVE WORK
BEAUTIFUL WORK
HURRAY FOR YOU
YOU TRIED HARD
YOU'RE SPECIAL
YOU'RE PERFECT
YOU'RE DARLING
REMARKABLE JOB
THAT'S CORRECT
YOU'RE THE BEST
YOU'RE SO SMART
GREAT DISCOVERY
YOU'RE A WINNER
SPECTACULAR JOB
YOU MADE MY DAY
YOU'RE WONDERFUL
YOU ARE EXCITING
YOU'RE IMPORTANT
YOU'RE BEAUTIFUL
I'M PROUD OF YOU
YOU'RE ON TARGET
YOU ARE EXCITING
HIP, HIP, HOORAY
YOU'RE IMPORTANT
YOU'RE FANTASTIC
YOU MAKE ME HAPPY

YOU'RE A TREASURE
BEAUTIFUL SHARING
YOU MAKE ME LAUGH
NOW YOU'RE FLYING
THAT'S INCREDIBLE
YOU'RE GROWING UP
YOU'RE INCREDIBLE
NOW YOU'VE GOT IT
WAY TO BE ON TASK
YOU'RE SENSATIONAL
YOU'RE CATCHING ON
YOU FIGURED IT OUT
THAT'S A GREAT JOB
YOU'RE CATCHING ON
YOU'RE ON YOUR WAY
YOU'RE THE GREATEST
YOU ARE RESPONSIBLE
WHAT AN IMAGINATION
YOU BRIGHTEN MY DAY
YOU'RE ON TOP OF IT
YOU'VE GOT A FRIEND
YOU MEAN A LOT TO ME
YOU'RE DOING SO WELL
YOU LEARNED IT RIGHT
YOU'RE A REAL TROUPER
A BIG HUG / A BIG KISS
I KNEW YOU COULD DO IT
EXCEPTIONAL PERFORMANCE
NOTHING CAN STOP YOU NOW

I LOVE YOU[2]

We need to delight in our children as God delights in His. To fail to touch our children in the variety of ways God has given is to make of them strangers.

Add your own encouraging words to the list above and pretty soon you'll be on a roll: Fabulous . . . What a star . . . You're so creative . . . You are such a blessing to me . . . What would I ever do without you . . . Stunning . . . Superb . . . Skyrockets. . . ."

And one last one: a good friend always says, "Sha sha!" which in the Neskapi Indian language simply means, "Go for it!"

---

² "100 Ways to Praise a Child," *Mark's Realm,* Webpage, Accessed: 5 May 2000, Updated: 15 March 2000, *http://www.sayno.com/child.html*

Chapter 6

GRIME AND PUNISHMENT

The kids are understandably a little nervous about this chapter, as I intend to reveal those few occasions when they broke the law.

It's only fair. I weigh 240 pounds, and they don't make a basket-case in my size. I have to have one custom-made. The kids, in a few isolated incidents, seemed all too eager to help.

I will maintain my children's anonymity, however, because I don't wish to unduly shame them. A good friend wishes to protect and defend, not expose. And the true friends that my sweet wife gave birth to have many times reminded me by their fine and responsible actions and their compassionate, loving ways how very poorly I sometimes measure up to their example.

IF YOU WANT YOUR CHILDREN TO BE YOUR GOOD FRIENDS INSTEAD OF YOUR CHIEF ADVERSARIES, BE A WITNESS FOR THEIR DEFENSE, NOT THEIR EXECUTIONER.

The best news of all is that each of us has been absolutely forgiven and our crimes blotted out by our chief confessor, Jesus Christ. In our house, we do not believe in dredging up past sins or in keeping accounts of wrongs committed. Forgiveness is a gentle ointment and a lasting cure. Use it lavishly and apply it liberally where your children are concerned, and a deep, appreciative friendship will be your reward.

If you're up against someone like Charlie Lowe, though, I wish you well.

Charlie was the only guy who ever made me want to commit murder. That deeply grieves me because to entertain murderous thoughts toward someone is, in fact, to commit murder in your heart. (See 1 John 3:15.) But Charlie was the type of guy who made a very convincing case for spontaneous birth. That's where there are no parents involved, just some stray mushroom spore that one day decides to mutate into a humanoid. It also decided to attend my junior high in southern California and torment me on a daily basis.

I had been raised to be kind, to return bad with good. I was a regular cheek-turner; I was, much like little Richie Petrie, the son on the old *Dick Van Dyke Show.* In one episode, Richie kept coming home with black eyes until his parents reluctantly said he could hit back. Come to find out, the bully was a girl who only wanted to kiss Richie, but he kept refusing.

I don't think that's what was on Charlie's mind.

He hit me to make me cry.

He hit me to make me wet my pants.

He hit me to embarrass me in front of my girlfriend, Faye.

I obliged him on all counts and inwardly seethed that I should be so belittled by someone a head shorter than I. But then, Faye was a head taller than I and two heads taller than Charlie. I was the cheese in the middle.

Nor did it help that my mom still called me Clinty and that when it came to buying pants, my chunky build was labeled "irregular husky." Why do clothiers do that to kids?

It didn't matter. There was another designation far more dreaded. Charlie called me "Kissy Kelly" because I still wore my jean cuffs turned up instead of in the newer, cooler straight-legged fashion. Mind you, we "irregular huskies" always had a good two feet of material left at the end of our legs, so there was no way we could go straight-legged, even if we wanted to. It never occurred to me that short Charlie probably had to buy his pants in the little boys' department. I could have made hay with that information. The trouble was, Charlie's blood-curdling sneer made up for his size and turned my brains to mush.

Charlie's henchmen were almost worse in their own way. They drew their strength from him, and if he had vanished, they would have deflated like used balloons. One we'll call Leech, the other Tick. Charlie didn't really treat them much better than he treated me, but he did share with them whatever he stole from me.

Leech and Tick didn't come from parents either. They were the spawn of forest-dwelling salamanders. So I plotted ever more delicious forms of mayhem for Charlie and his performing amphibians. In truth, they only robbed me, beat me, and stalked me for fun. As for me, I murdered them a hundred times over in my heart.

Such is the private anguish of a child. But murder is a capital offense, and I was a candidate for death row. Jesus changed all that, and I now wish Charlie no ill. What I do wish is that my waist size would descend below my inseam length just once before I die. I confess to you that I have broken all of the Ten Commandments (some just in my mind, of course) at one time or another and am a condemned criminal apart from Christ. In Him, my sentence has been commuted, and I am a free man!

Thus, being friends with your children does not mean siding with them no matter what the situation. It does mean calling to mind their great value in God's economy and letting them know that they are worth every minute of sleeplessness and every fallen tear that it takes to put them back on track.

I remember the time when one of our children filled a customer's birdbath with gasoline while doing his paper route. Next, the garage was entered and gasoline was poured on the floor and some rolls of carpet. And this wasn't the first time. No matches, thank God, but why this?

The answer, after much soul-searching, was a pitiful, "To see if I could get away with it."

Unprovoked malice from a kid with no history of delinquent behavior didn't make sense. This was the nice-as-pie, church-going child who wouldn't hurt the proverbial flea.

> PRAISE AN HONEST CHILD WITH, "IT TOOK A LOT OF COURAGE TO TELL ME THE TRUTH WHEN YOU KNEW I'D BE MAD."

Would this evil derail this kid of ours? Not if two of his closest friends—his mother and I—had anything to do with it. We did not defend, side with, or make excuses for this ten-year-old whom we had raised to fear God and love all mankind. We did not spank, ground, or withhold privileges (tried and true options in other circumstances). What we did was considerably more difficult.

The three of us drove to the lady's house and arrived the same time as the police, fire marshal, and pumper truck with crew. The authorities investigated the crime and found that gas fumes had come within a gnat's whisker of igniting from the electric motor on the meat freezer. They confronted the child with the terrible truth of what could have happened in the resulting explosion.

They also questioned the child's integrity, character, and responsibility and frisked him for matches. Had there been any, it would have spelled arson and even deeper trouble. They wanted to take photos of the child and build a file, but Mom Kelly refused. That didn't stop the questions.

Was there a history of delinquency? Did the child know who else might have been placed in danger because a fire crew was busy responding to a vandalism call? They were tough on our child, and we were glad they were. However, Cheryll protected her young from the full onslaught of authority. Did they have to be that rough on a first-time offender? We ached to hug, kiss, and protect more, but the music had to be faced.

When the authorities were done, the child had to face the grown daughter of the elderly lady who lived alone in the house and always paid her newspaper bill on time. How kindly she explained the fear her mother had experienced, not knowing who it was who kept doing those things to her house. She never wanted to believe that it was her sweet, friendly paper carrier, except that the vandalism always occurred right after a delivery.

Then it was time to face the elderly lady herself. The child wept bitterly and apologized that never in a million years had the possibility of an explosion come to mind. The two of them hugging together in the yard, framed by firemen and fire fighting equipment, was an amazing sight. She started to cry, and in the tears we all shed was forgiveness and restoration.

But it wasn't over by a long way. Our insurance company paid six hundred dollars in damages. The entire Kelly family went to the fire station and talked with the fire marshal about the incredible dangers of fire. He debated bringing out the "heavy artillery"—photos of actual burn victims. We said he should and he did. It was a gruesome object lesson in how horribly a prank can escalate.

When the offending child was able at last to weigh all the time, effort, expense, risk, and emotional suffering that resulted, what a toll! To have personal character questioned, Christian witness mocked, and family name shamed was a triple judgment. The result was a toughening of the child's fiber far longer-lasting than any "lesson" we might have devised.

Again, as we do when any evil attempts to tear this family in two, the six of us went to our knees in the living room. Confession, prayer, weeping, and great gobs of forgiveness slathered on the sin-wounded child spoke volumes:

"God is faithful to forgive."

"Tell Him what you did wrong and the load will lift."

"When one Kelly falls, all suffer; when a Kelly repents, all rejoice."

"Your family are your dearest friends; though we know all your warts, and you know ours, we love you more fiercely than anyone outside these walls."

"Our loyalty towards each other is a certainty in an uncertain world."

When I was on the board of a ministry to children trapped by the occult, I heard heart-rending stories of kids with no security, no safety net, and no network of loving support. It had been communicated to them in a thousand different ways that they were worthless and fit only for evil and vice. Abused by parents and other family members, their innocence and trust destroyed, they willingly embraced whatever evil had to offer.

SAY TO YOUR

CHILD, "NO

MATTER WHAT

HAPPENS, I'M IN

YOUR CORNER!"

What do you communicate to your children? In the face of their grime, crime, or slime, do you turn away? Do you reinforce their feelings of worthlessness by your words? Or does your speech, your body language, and your lifestyle communicate the same message as Jesus gave to the adulterous woman He saved from stoning, **"neither do I condemn you," Jesus declared. "Go now and leave your life of sin"** (John 8:11)?

My children know they are my friends because I think highly of them, I respect them, and I do not condemn them. I know full well that with God's help, they can rise above evil. But I must communicate that trust, and there's no better time than when they're caught red-handed.

When a couple of the kids had a brief fling with shoplifting, Cheryll and I did the normal agonizing. Where had *we* gone wrong? Who were they hanging out with? What were they lacking? Is it the stock market, a full moon, or *what?*

You know how parents get. *Berzerk-a-rama.*

Then comes the cold water in the face when you're forced to visualize your son or daughter in the store, glancing furtively over their shoulders before slipping a chocolate bar into a pocket or a purse.

A chocolate bar, for crying out loud! They practically live in Candyland, yet they steal chocolate bars. Go figure. And while you're at it, tell me why I shoplifted a paperback book when I was seventeen. I had a library card and access to thousands of volumes in the greatest free lending system in the world, yet I broke the law for a $1.95 paperback.

Why? Because I am a sinner and wanted to see if I could beat the system. I was never caught, yet the book brought me no pleasure. The theft was a beggarly triumph because my best friends, my parents, had thought highly enough of me to communicate that it was beneath me as a child of God to transgress the law. By stealing, I had chosen to eat the cast-off of swine. I should expect an upset stomach.

Thankfully, Cheryll and I have raised four children who get queasy over sin. I like to call it "spiritual genetics."

Come, my children, listen to me; I will teach you the fear of the LORD.
—Psalm 34:11

In the end, King David was glad it was discovered that he had committed adultery with Bathsheba. He was grateful for a broken spirit, a broken and contrite heart before God. (See Psalm 51:17.) "Besides," says Steph, "it's too much trouble to have to face a family meeting, confess everything in front of everyone, and use up all that Kleenex." Hey, if an emotional gauntlet works, use an emotional gauntlet.

The acid of guilt should burn so badly that they are driven to confess to gain relief. Then when they sin, they will bungle it. You want to raise inept sinners. It is those who are able to finesse their sins who are in greatest spiritual peril.

YOUR KIDS WILL BE AMONG YOUR CLOSEST FRIENDS IF YOU PLANT WITHIN THEM A HIGHLY DEVELOPED SENSE OF RIGHT AND WRONG.

You will never experience friendship from a child you have taught to excuse sin or to cover it up—as do the sitcom families on television—as a sign of clever wits. Because they cannot respect your deviousness, they will spend their lives attempting to outwit and outdeceive you. Instead of making a friend, you will have created a blood adversary.

The police department in Houston, Texas, sums up what *not* to do in "Twelve Rules for Raising Delinquent Children":[1]

---

[1] Source unkown.

1. Begin in infancy to give the child everything he wants. In this way, he will grow up to believe the world owes him a living.

2. When he picks up bad words, laugh at him. This will make him think he's cute.

3. Never give him any spiritual training. Wait until he is twenty-one and then let him "decide for himself."

4. Avoid use of the word "wrong." It may develop a guilt complex. This will condition him to believe later, when he is arrested for stealing a car, that society is against him and he is being persecuted.

5. Pick up everything he leaves lying around. Do everything for him so that he will be experienced in throwing all responsibility on others.

6. Let him read any printed matter he can get his hands on. Be careful that the silverware and drinking glasses are sterilized, but let his mind feast on garbage.

7. Quarrel frequently in the presence of your children. In this way they won't be so shocked when the home is broken up later.

8. Give a child all the spending money he wants. Never let him earn his own.

9. Satisfy his every craving for food, drink, and comfort. See that every sensual desire is gratified.

10. Take his part against neighbors, teachers, and policemen. They are all prejudiced against your child.

11. When he gets into real trouble, apologize for yourself by saying, "I never could do anything with him."

12. Prepare for a life of grief. You will be likely to have it.

Teaching right from wrong means that you will have to be scrupulous. No sneaking in under the circus tent. When the sign says your sixteen-year-old must pay adult prices, that's the price you pay even if the child can pass for fifteen. When the speed limit says fifty-five miles per hour, don't justify doing sixty-five. When the cashier gives you too much change, take it back. When you have committed a wrong, take full responsibility rather than attempt to worm your way out or to put a more flattering "spin" on it. In that way, you communicate that righteous people live righteously. They sweat the small stuff. If not, you permit a "fudge factor" that will distort your children's view of morality.

READ THE NEWSPAPER WITH YOUR CHILDREN, ASKING THEM TO POINT OUT THE CONSEQUENCES OF SIN AND A GODLESS LIFE.

When you do your taxes, show your children income and outgo and what deductions your family is entitled to and why. When you vote, take the time to explain the pros and cons of your candidate. When you read the paper, ask your kids' opinions about questionable events and morally ambiguous decisions made.

By including your children in the daily flow of life, you exercise their moral faculties and cause them to wrestle early with larger issues of right and wrong. Then, when the department store calls to say your son or daughter has been shoplifting, you will have a broader base for helping them and the family through rough waters.

The store management was hard in their treatment of our offending child, and we're glad they were. It didn't matter that it was only a couple of forty-cent candy bars. Here again, it is critical to make it clear that there are no small crimes. Entertain sin of any size and a person becomes desensitized to all sin.

We struggled with the one-hundred-dollar fine for eighty cents worth of candy and the cold, accusatory letter from department store headquarters demanding the fine be paid quickly. It was very difficult for our child, our friend, to feel branded as a thief and to have brought shame upon the family. But again, that child's five closest friends—all family—rallied around and prayerfully and lovingly picked up the fallen one.

Considering that the wages of sin are eternal death, a hundred dollars was a paltry sum to have to pay. Again, each of us was reminded that the gift of God is eternal life, and we do not have to suffer the bitter defeat of death for our sin. Jesus Christ took our sins and conquered the death we deserve. We are free indeed. (See John 8:36.)

Another child was quite young when he lifted a wallet one Christmas season. The store personnel didn't know, but we did not cover for him, let it drop, or take the wallet back ourselves. I took the child back to the store, and he had to muster the courage to face the clerk and confess what he had done. Because of his young age, she forgave him and did not press charges. What was at stake—what is always at stake—were principles of honesty, respect, personal responsibility, and the choice to live a life of lawbreaking or law-abiding.

> PUT WASHED QUARTERS IN YOUR CHILD'S BIRTHDAY CAKE AND LET EVERYONE KNOW THERE'S A SURPRISE IN IT. IT SETS THAT CAKE APART FROM ALL OTHERS AND SAYS, "HERE'S A LITTLE SOMETHING EXTRA FOR AN EXTRAORDINARY KID."

So in its own small but significant way, the tableau of family closing ranks about the wounded one is a picture of divine grace at work. They are not there to excuse the wrong, but to rescue and restore the wrongdoer. As Jesus prevented the mob from casting the first stone, friends in the family are there to keep the rocks from reaching the accused. Condemnation is lifted. Healing is well underway.

What we're saying as a family of friends is that no matter what you've done, you have great worth here. We're no more perfect than you, and each of us knows that when any one of us falls or is hurting, the rest will be there. What an amazing source of strength and comfort!

We like to observe a special birthday tradition of hiding quarters in the cake. At our house every birthday, the honoree gets to choose the kind of cake they want. Before the cake is frosted, clean quarters are hidden inside. Anyone finding a quarter in their piece must declare the discovery with a vigorous "Eureka!" in order to keep it. The cake is good, but the quarters make it extra special. So it is with one another. We let our children know that we are always eagerly on the lookout for the shiny silver surprises in them and that those far outweigh the mistakes and sins common to us all.

Have we punished our kids when they've misbehaved? Sure. We've dished out everything from revoked telephone privileges to writing one thousand times, "I will not talk back to my father." But more importantly, we have tried to teach our children that we are all living epistles. That's what Paul called the Corinthian believers. (See 2 Corinthians 3:2 KJV.) We are flesh-and-blood letters of recommendation that the faith is authentic.

It doesn't mean there won't be the occasional misspelling, but your family, your friends, ought to be there to help edit the typos of sin from your life.

Grime-fighters, that's what we are. It's a dirty job, but that's what friends are for.

Chapter 7

BUDDING SEXUALITY
AND HOW TO NIP IT

There's nothing quite as romantic as hearing your wife say, "I didn't start itching until you got home."

Cheryll's such a kidder.

It gave us great pleasure to sit down with our kids on our twentieth wedding anniversary and explain to them how Cheryll and I became best of friends. Oh, how the world bombards them at every bend by endless reference to what's "sexy." It's up to us to tell them that the chemistry alone will blow up in their faces. What makes for family and home is deep friendship. My wife and I have to model that before our children can go out and handle the elements of love without injury.

They listened intently to the tape of our wedding ceremony. There was the trumpet fanfare from "The Prince of Denmark March," Pastor Glen Cole singing "The Lord's Prayer," their mother and father, no older than our youngest is now, exchanging the age-old vows of "I do"!

As I am now twice the man I used to be, the ring that used to slide easily off my finger must now be pried loose, but finally I was able to read for them the inscription written inside: "God is our eternal love." As giddy and starry-eyed as we were in 1971, we knew that without that foundation, we would make an utter mess of it.

As long as I live, I will never write any words more profound than those five.

We told the children for years that young as they were, they should pray for their future spouses. Sure, at the time those spouses may have only been ten, twelve, or sixteen years old, but wouldn't it be exciting if they in turn had been praying for their future mates too? Life with God is an exhilarating partnership, and it's never too soon to take a more active part in it.

BEGIN NOW PRAYING WITH YOUR CHILDREN FOR THEIR FUTURE SPOUSES.

I like the Jim Rutz approach. Jim's a Christian, a writer, and a business consultant who wanted a wife. He took out a full-page ad in *Christian Contemporary Music* magazine (March 1987, inside back of mailing wrapper), and he did it in style. Above a photo of Jim in a suit of armor standing next to a white charger was the headline: **Damsel Wanted (Distress Optional).**

He described himself as having "blue eyes . . . golden retriever brown hair . . . politics to the right of Genghis Khan . . . special interests: prayer, music, language . . . sports: running for endurance, racquetball for exercise, golf for fun, chess for blood," and a propensity for collies, rain, in-depth Bible studies, and old Bogart movies.

He said that as a successful dragon-slayer, he was looking for a fair ladyship who was spiritually mature and liked to be pampered yet desired to be challenged, supported, and loved. He promised to answer all letters and send a collection of the ten greatest poems of all time.

The response form said in part, "Dear Jim, I'm sending you this coupon because I can't stand lonely knights. . . . I'm not too sure about you, but I like your horse. . . . " Then came a place for lady in waiting (name), abode (address), and shire (city, state, zip). He also offered a trip for two to Europe for anyone who introduced him to the maiden he would eventually marry. Now that's class.

I've never met Jim Rutz. I don't know if in his case it paid to advertise. But I do know that that ad speaks of a zest for life and its adventures that we were meant to have.

We must reinforce for our children the biblical mandate to serve our God, to seek after His righteousness, to shed light on this earth while we're here, and to file for citizenship in the eternal kingdom of heaven through Jesus Christ. If I am gifted with romance and the desire to give myself to another individual, then I should eagerly seek how to do that in a way that is true and pleasing.

That quest begins at home. I saw it in my grandparents the time Grandfather poured scalding coffee down my grandmother's pants at Yosemite National Park. Of course, he never meant to. She was sitting on the ground enjoying the view and he was pouring a cup of coffee from a thermos. The thermos slipped, the cup tipped, and Grandmother flipped!

While I was not prepared to see my granny's girdle as quickly as I did, neither did I overlook the tenderness with which Grandfather nursed both her blisters and her anguish. Soon they were lost in their own little world of need expressed and need met, speaking quietly and lovingly together, my grandmother's discomfort and embarrassment washing away in the gentle ministrations of her life companion. All those years they had been married—I could see why.

The two greatest memories I have of my grandfather are the way he treated Grandma and the fact that he worked for Heinz 57 and brought me neat little plastic pickle whistles in the shape of baby gherkins.

Again, I saw the tenderness of one mate for another when my father lay in the hospital bed in our living room dying of cancer. With just a couple more months to live, that big, strapping, hard-working muscle of a man drooped helpless as a baby. Mom never left him and rarely complained. Though they could not speak of the malignancy putting an end to their romance, with every dip of a washcloth or spoon of food, they silently broadcast their love.

We must tell our children that God will honor their faithfulness no matter how many times they have seen marriages go bad, no matter how many friends they know from broken homes, no matter the pattern of brokenness in their own home. All the bad news and marital failure rates amount to self-fulfilling prophecies.

TELL YOUR CHILDREN HOW WONDERFUL YOUR SPOUSE IS. THAT LOVE WHICH YOU TWO SHARE WILL WASH OVER THEM.

Fidelity. What a lovely word. To remain faithful to an obligation or trust. To remain steadfast in the face of any temptation to renounce, desert, or betray. But far from being a dusty, dry duty, fidelity speaks of zeal, devotion, and allegiance. Remember the old hi-fi stereo? "High fidelity" sound was the manufacturer's way of saying that a new height had been achieved in the exactness of recorded sound, an incomparable integrity was used to capture the original performance.

I cried tears of wonder and joy as I described for our children the incredible fidelity of their mother. Her faithfulness to me fortifies and enriches my faithfulness to her. No matter how tired, bored, jaded, or irritated we have become with people, circumstances, or even each other in now twenty-nine years of marriage vow-keeping, it is that astonishing *trust* that keeps us in love.

It is the same trust that we have in the children and they have in us. Once, through a mix-up in communication, we forgot our youngest child and left him at night in a downtown tennis court. Another time we were delayed getting home by a couple of hours, and our eight-year-old was locked out and had no way of knowing what had happened to us. On those thankfully rare occasions, those kids knew the terror of contemplating that their parents, for whatever reasons, had abandoned them. *Is it over? Don't they care anymore? Are they never coming back?*

Being the cause of those agonies ought to haunt every parent. Sexual abuse, domestic violence, indifference, and infidelity come when the parents intentionally break trust, when it no longer matters. Do you rush to heal the break, even the hairline fracture, or do you leave it to widen and crumble? Whatever the cost, you must restore fidelity with the family you have been given. If children observe their mom and dad mistreating fidelity in the marriage relationship or the parent-child bond, they will rapidly experience a meltdown of their own personal standards of excellence and allegiance.

GIVE 'EM A WINK AND SAY, "YOU ARE GOD'S REWARD TO ME FOR EATING ALL MY PEAS!"

How wonderfully reassuring it is for them to see us holding hands, poking and tickling one another, rubbing one another's shoulders or feet, and making the effort to slip away for a three-day "mini-moon" now and then. How good it is to gather them up into our arms and slow dance around the kitchen as a threesome or to make a "kid sandwich" with one of them caught in the squeeze. Sometimes Cheryll and I will gang up on one of the children and tag team our way through a wrestling laugh-a-thon. No one's wet their pants yet, but we've come close.

Sure, the kids wrinkle up their faces at our childish antics and displays of romantic affection, but we witness the twinkle in their eyes that says, "You two love and enjoy each other, and that love washes over us." When Steph left for college, she gave me a note with a PS that read, "Thanks for loving Mom *soo* much. Some of the qualities I look for in a boyfriend I see in you!"

We've never kept from the kids how they got here. We made it clear early on that they are wanted, intentional human beings. No, we did not keep ovulation charts or plot earnings potential to determine frequency and size of family. We did not test for the baby's sex nor did we color coordinate every bootie and diaper pin. They did come girl, boy, girl, boy, and whenever that fact is noted in public, I will arch my eyebrows and grin idiotically as if that were somehow an indicator of expert family planning. But no, we just kind of let nature take its course. We talked about a baseball team, but Cheryll's bone structure meant that she had to have all her babies Caesarean. "Four max," said the doctor. Four max it was.

Occasionally, in jest, one kid will accuse another of being adopted and therefore not as entitled to "the family's millions." (Millions of what? Bug bites? Dust balls?) Only Nate seems to have taken it to heart. After all, the other three were "stairsteps," one year apart. He came along three-and-a-half years after his closest sibling. "Doesn't that mean I was an accident, a surprise?" he'll ask.

We try to remind him that each and every child is a gift of God and that when you are a child of God, whatever happens in your life

TELL YOUR

INQUISITIVE

CHILD, "YOU

KNOW, YOU ASK

THE BEST

QUESTIONS. I'M SO

GLAD YOU'RE

CURIOUS AND

AREN'T AFRAID

TO ASK!"

work[s] **together for good** (Romans 8:28 KJV, insert mine). We tell him we spent three-and-a-half years gathering our breath and strength, for we knew we could have just one more child and we wanted that one to be the finishing touch.

Sex ed occurs at home and it too ought to be intentional. My father was extremely awkward in discussing the matter, and I can remember only one official sex session when we pulled to the side of the road, and he gulped his way through an explanation full of euphemisms. The talk was pretty sketchy and probably raised more questions than it answered, but I'm grateful I received that much given the day and age.

I've tried to do more than that with my boys, and Cheryll with the girls. Beyond the mechanics of sex, which really are fairly simple and straightforward, we've spent far more time discussing the gift of sexuality and the great part it plays in fulfilling God's intentions for the earth. To be fruitful and multiply, to raise up souls to praise God, bring illumination into society, and populate heaven, is to take a direct hand in building the kingdom of God.

Sex ed meant telling Shane that having children of light actually helps neutralize the godless pollution in the world. There is no more profound thing you can say to your child than, "The kids you raise, as the kids we've raised, will have an impact for God on generations to come."

Sex ed meant telling Nate that sex, contrary to all the hype, is not a plaything or a mere physical release the same as any other bodily function. Sex ed is hearing him tell me, "Sex is for marriage because that pleases God."

Sex ed is telling the kids about the apostle Paul's sex ed discussion with the people of Corinth. First Corinthians 6:12-20 is one of the clearest explanations of the inseparable link between a person's sexual health and their spiritual health. To remain sexually pure, to stay a virgin until marriage, and to express sexuality only within marriage is to honor God with one's body. To love, honor, and enjoy God is the chief purpose of mankind.

> *Fear God and keep his commandments, for this is the whole duty of man.*
> —Ecclesiastes 12:13

> *Now, O Israel, what does the LORD your God ask of you but to fear the LORD your God, to walk in all his ways, to love him, to serve the LORD your God with all your heart and with all your soul.*
> —Deuteronomy 10:12

Sex ed is telling my boys that even four kids later, I don't have all the answers to sex. I don't know why puberty hits so young and children are capable of producing other children at twelve and thirteen years of age. I don't know why their sex drive kicks in at so tender an age when they can't and shouldn't do anything to express it. I don't know why men are so quickly aroused sexually, at times by things not even remotely connected. I don't know why some women suffer PMS irritability or why a husband and wife's sexual desires and intensity can be so different.

WHEN YOUR CHILDREN MAKE WISE DECISIONS, PRAISE THEM FOR RISING TO SUCH A LEVEL OF MATURITY.

Sex ed is letting my kids know that I know how utterly frustrating it is to be attracted to someone of the opposite sex, including a sexual attraction, when they are far too young and immature—and unemployed—to make a lasting personal pledge to that individual.

Sex ed is struggling upstream against the flash flood of "sexiness" washing down from the arid hills of movies, books, television, and pop music. It takes a strong swimmer to turn off, tune out, and screen that which enters our souls through the eye and ear ports. When a television character declares that "a man is a lot of things, but he's not a virgin," I can turn to my boys and ask, "Is that statement true or false?" I know what their answer will be, that they truly believe in being virgins—not because it's an easy thing to be but because they are firmly convinced that God knows best. I must feed my kids and encourage them to feed on wholesome, restoring, redeeming material, especially the Bible, so that they build a habit of reaching for that first.

We laughed ruefully with our older kids because they were an "oppressed minority" in America. They were part of the 30 percent or so of American teens who had not had sex with another person by their senior year in high school. We joked how they ought to march on Washington and demand "Virgin Rights." A sad thing to joke about, I know, but our kids could practice "oral contraception" by saying no and still be winsome individuals whom others admire and secretly envy for their virginity.

No, it is not easy. They were and are attractive, active, compassionate kids, who are naturally loving and who like to express their love. They must be on their guard, and so must Mom and Dad be on theirs.

It is especially subtle when sex comes disguised as sensitivity, affection, and comfort. One kiss of "I appreciate you, and you mean a lot to me," can lead to another of "I need something more, something deeper than just friends." On the one hand, we have encouraged our kids to be loving, supportive friends who easily throw an arm around one another. How good it is to see them praying, holding, and crying with someone who needs to know the loving touch of God expressed by a child of God. On the other hand, we need to guide them in how to gauge the intensity of their emotions, how to discern the nature of their relationships, and how to detect even a slight change in the temperature of physical feelings.

We don't do this by holding classes. In the thousand and one daily details from infancy on up, they develop their personal patterns and response to others. The Kellys have always been an emotional, high-touch bunch. At the same time, we have practiced what the church in medieval times called *puritas cordis,* or "transparency of the heart." Monks practiced it in being single-mindedly focused on God with thoughts and actions that were a reflection of that devotion. Each was required to work a plot of land as an act of worship that brought them in closer communion with the Lord. Members of a family should also be transparent with each other. In that way, we become attuned to one another, and as soon as one member is out of tune, the rest know it. Whereas you need to be clear-headed before making a major purchase, you need to be clear-hearted before facing a challenge of the glands.

CATCH YOUR CHILD'S EYE ACROSS A CROWDED ROOM OR ON THE PLAYING FIELD AND GIVE THEM A WINK AND THE THUMBS UP SIGN.

How any father survives the constant shelling of the home by exploding hormones is sometimes a mystery to me. Some take cover in their work, staying at the office until all hours. Some stuff a twenty-dollar bill in their son's hand and say, "Have a good time." Still others throw frequent pity parties at the local tavern. Men don't seem especially well equipped to halt the sap when it's fixing to flow.

One spring night, I was enjoying a delightful slumber when Cheryll woke me up. The three things my wife says at times like these that turn my blood to ice are:

1) "Are you sitting down?"

2) "Please don't hate me when I tell you this."

3) "Honey, are you asleep?"

Any one of them spells intense trouble, but when used all at the same time, you just know the lynch mob is closing in fast, and the noose they're carrying has your name on it.

I don't know about you, but my guard tends to be down a little at two in the morning. Fortunately, on this occasion Cheryll used only one of the above sayings, number three I believe. I mumbled, "Of course I wasn't asleep, my sweet, but working tirelessly on the floor plan for our little cabana in Jamaica."

She huffed, "Hardly!" (a fourth thing she says that I don't particularly care for) and gave me a little shake. I listened as she explained that our son was waiting in the living room after having just returned from an unauthorized trip to the convenience store in our new van.

We moved to the living room where our son sat looking deeply disturbed with himself. We talked for a while about trust and responsibility and, as always, he saw the pack of troubles unleashed by one seemingly small, but rash, decision on his part. We do not take deception lightly.

But that wasn't all that troubled him. He further confessed that he had been doing this every now and then for a couple of weeks in order to visit a new girlfriend after hours on school nights. His need to be with her had superseded all other considerations of our trust, her parents' trust, and even her trust in their friendship. She had told him not to break the rules, but he had done it anyway.

He had told us that this was to have been a more casual summer friendship that would have to end when he started college. But his after-hour visitations had taken the friendship to a new level. He was giving her cause to believe there was more to this friendship than a summer acquaintance. He asked what I thought he should do about his girlfriend. Given the circumstances under which their relationship had developed, I advised that the right thing to do was to end it and just be friends. He nodded slowly and a little reluctantly, but agreed.

There was a lot of soul-searching that night (ending somewhere around 5:00 A.M.). We spoke of how many of his few times of real trouble had come over girls, including a broken nose. We talked of respect for parents and for himself. We considered how little he might really think of the relationship to use it in the way he had. We also praised God that our son was open with us about things that we would not have known if he had not told us. And as grateful as we are that none of the kids have taken to drugs, theft, or promiscuity, we asked the good Lord to teach us again that sin is sin and must not be entertained in any form.

INSTEAD OF CALLING YOUR CHILD "A REAL CHARACTER", SAY, "YOU'RE A KID WITH CHARACTER!" WATCH YOUR CHILD RISE TO THE COMPLIMENT!

There were a good many tears that night as the three of us lamented our sin and shortcomings. If it was so easy to rationalize deceit in the "little things," how difficult could it be to rationalize sexual intercourse with a girlfriend or other misuses of God's creation? To struggle against the lure of pornography or the snare of masturbation, even to fall to them, is not the end. God can always work with the contrite but imperfect heart of the one wrestling with holiness. But to stop caring, to become anesthetized to sin, is a horror. **"Blessed are those who mourn, for they will be comforted"** (Matthew 5:4). What is it that they mourn over? They mourn over their sin! That is the kind of "transparency of the heart" God can build kingdoms with.

Chaucer, the English literary great, writes in his *Canterbury Tales* about a fat, self-indulgent clergyman who in his derision Chaucer calls "a prelate fit for exhibition," an exhibition of shame. But what our son and his mother and I rediscovered in the small hours before dawn was that God wants to make of us an exhibition of righteousness, a public display of His redemptive handiwork. How quickly we can find ourselves in the wrong when we allow our hormones to strut their stuff uncontrolled.

"Be at war with your vices, at peace with your neighbors, and let every year find you a better man." Ben Franklin's advice is no truer than where our sexuality is concerned. When your children begin to bud in the birds and bees department, don't panic. Remember that birds build nests and bees make honey. Sex as intended is neither sinister nor fatal.

Rather than attempting to deny it, kill it, or goad it into rage, channel your children's passion—talk about it, pray over it. Lift weights with your sons, get a family pass to the "Y," or encourage them to take second jobs, but whatever it takes, don't let it go unchecked. They must see their sexuality as one of the solid building blocks God uses for His glory.

It takes a true friend who is willing to show them.

Chapter 8

DO DELIGHTFUL DATES COME FROM SWEATY PALMS?

She was the perfect date—cute and beautiful at the same time. Her smile radiated warmth and acceptance and a total interest in everything I said and did.

I could have said "ripe cucumbers," and she would have giggled musically. "Five pounds for a dollar" would send her into gales of melodious laughter. I can't even imagine the response had I said, "Will that be paper or plastic?"

She sat by my side, her warm, delicate hand in mine. Those gorgeous eyes sparkled and danced, and a bushel of radiant brown hair swirled and shimmered in the late summer sun.

We stopped to pick blackberries by the side of the road. With slender fingers she popped the sweet warm fruit into my mouth and playfully dabbed at a trickle of purple juice that escaped down my chin. When at last we arrived at the outdoor Snoqualmie Falls Forest Theater and took our seats beneath the trees, I had fallen in love all over again.

Stephanie was eight years old and I was thirty-two. A bit of an age gap, but what does it matter when you are father and daughter and you're out on a date?

Compare that with only my second date in high school when Julie asked me to go to the Sadie Hawkins Dance. Never mind that my palms went sweaty at the thought or that I danced like the hippos in *Fantasia*. She thought it would be sweet if we dressed really different from everyone else. No Lil' Abner or Daisy Mae were we to be. Oh, no.

We went as a burlap sack.

That is no misprint. The two of us went as one sack. Horizontal, closed at both ends, holes for arms.

There we were: she the right hand, I the left. Everywhere she went, I was forced to follow and vice versa. Have you ever spent an entire evening with someone you barely know in four feet of sack without letting your inside arms touch? Talk about stress! And something neither of us thought of, brilliant planners that we were, was what would happen when one-half of the bag had to go to the bathroom? The topic never came up the entire evening, but neither did we go near the punch bowl.

One other interesting tidbit of burlap sack trivia: When you turn a corner fast and you're the inside person, plant your feet firmly while twisting your shoulders in the direction of the turn. Centrifugal force will whip your date around the bend just like on a roller rink. The whole night, I kept an eye out for left-hand turns.

Eventually, Julie caught on and immediately looked for a right-hand turn. Once, when we came to the end of the hallway, we nearly tore our sack in two. One other word of caution—if you stand your ground too long on a turn, you will meet your date head-on; start forward too soon before your date has completely negotiated the turn, and the two of you will fly off in the direction of the skid. Remember these defensive driving tips, and you should get many safe miles out of your burlap sack.

To this day, I date my children individually two or three times a year. As well as they have worked as a foursome, they need to be recognized and enjoyed individually for the unique gifts and talents they bring to the family. Besides, they never turn me down.

What a thrill to hear a busy college freshman daughter say, "You bet, Dad! Let me get that on my calendar right now." Could that be the same Stephanie who held my hand in the forest a decade ago, who joined in the hunt for garter snakes just before curtain time?

"You oughtta hear my college friends when I tell 'em I'm going out with my dad," says Steph with a grin. "They go, 'What! You mean you want to?'"

Close friends with your dad. What a concept!

Our kids enjoy our company and our creative juice, and we enjoy theirs. They've never been ashamed to be seen with us or to invite us to chaperone dances and choir outings. One day in his senior year at high school, my oldest son invited me to spend the entire day with him. I took a vacation day from work, attended every class period, ate lunch in the cafeteria, and even took part in a discussion on marriage and family in health class. Of course, I had to raise my hand first.

"KIDNAP" YOUR CHILDREN FROM BED ON A SATURDAY MORNING AND TREAT THEM TO BREAKFAST AT A RESTAURANT.

Dates with your kids are a refreshing break from the routine, and you can customize them to the particular personality and interests of the child you're dating. With Steph, it is hamburger joints, shopping sprees, and music concerts. With Shane, it's music stores, pizza parlors, and improvisational comedy clubs. With Amy, it's Mexican food, volleyball tournaments, and love stories on the silver screen. With Nate, it's video parlors, fishing trips, and ice cream sundaes.

You will be caught by pleasant surprises along the way. I took Shane to a writers' conference in Idaho, and we ended up on the floor of the air terminal reading humorous verse to each other out of Calvin Miller's *The Aardvark Parked on the Ark*. I took Stephanie to a Whitney Houston concert, and we had a lively discussion about Whitney's profession of Christian faith and the obvious adulation secular stardom brings. I took Nate deep-sea fishing for bass, and we lay in a tent listening to old Groucho Marx comedy routines. I took Amy to a restaurant that looked like the inside of a trapper's cabin, and we drove ourselves nuts trying to solve interlocking metal puzzles.

SHARE A SPECIAL PLACE WITH YOUR CHILD WHERE ONLY THE TWO OF YOU GO.

On dates with my kids I've watched monster trucks battle for supremacy; jugglers juggle fish, bowling balls, and a loaf of bread; and *The Muppets Take Manhattan*. One of my sons has rowed me around a lake; one daughter has gotten me into a hundred-foot glass elevator (plastered against the back wall); and I have eaten in an Irish pub, a Greek cabaret, an Italian bistro, and an Indian longhouse.

We have always had fun getting away from the "crowd" of family and school for a little one-on-one attention. It's like any group of friends. You love being together, but isn't it nice to get away with that one special friend to find out how they're doing inside and what they're thinking?

Teenage Shane and I went to Seattle one warm spring evening in May. Quite unexpectedly, we heard the wonderfully brassy sounds of a Latin band in the distance. When we got there, we found a celebration of *Cinco de Mayo*, Mexican Independence Day, in full swing. I hoisted Shane on my shoulders, and we swayed and moved to the happy beat for probably the better part of two hours. As night fell, the lights came on and the festivities carried us away. We could hardly hear each other, and yet just feeling the music and experiencing the magic of the festival together made that one of the best dates we've ever had.

Once, Amy and I toured the Seattle Art Gallery. In ninety minutes we visited Africa, China, Egypt, and much of Europe. We exclaimed over the intricacies of jade and ivory, the subtleties of oils and watercolors, and the bold earthiness of clay and reed. Afterwards, we went to a waterfront restaurant and pored over a wall of autographed photos of celebrities who had dined where we dined. The evening was fun and quite out of the ordinary for both of us.

We still laugh about the menu. Amy wanted to review the restaurant for her school paper and asked the waiter if she could have a menu to take home. He looked hesitant for a moment, then said he'd be right back. We were thinking a small take-out menu to go, but instead, he brought one of the full-sized, fancy, plastic-bound ones and said that while he probably shouldn't give it away, in her case he'd make an exception. He proceeded to fold it and told her to put it in her purse. She's still amazed that a high school restaurant critic carried that much clout!

Shane and I took off for an overnighter to the Oregon coast. One of the most pleasant surprises was a tiny little playhouse in Lincoln City. Here we discovered a deliciously funny play called *Everybody Loves Opal*. Opal is a bag lady with a heart of gold who turns the tables on some would-be crooks. We bought our tickets late and were at first sandwiched into a tiny little "orchestra pit." However, as curtain time approached and there were a couple of no-shows, we were reseated front and center in two of the best seats in the house.

Pretending that popcorn is your caviar and the soft drinks are of a particularly fine carbonated vintage, you don't have to worry about bonding with your kids. Personalize your relationship with each of your children, and they won't drift away in the storms of adolescence and puberty—or when midlife strikes you! These things can drive a wedge of estrangement between parent and child unless you have built a reserve of friendship to neutralize the urges and surges of life.

We are often so busy guiding, correcting, and, sigh, pushing our children into responsible personhood, we forget to say, "I'm all yours. What would *you* like to do?"

In those years when your kids *want* your attention, let them have it. When I started my new job at Seattle Pacific University, Nate fashioned me a pink gavel out of clay. It was my "office-warming" gift. I was appreciative but must have looked a little puzzled at that particular choice. My then nine-year-old, with the wisdom of the ages, explained, "You're the new guy, Dad. Nobody's going to listen to you at first. When you can't seem to get their attention, use this gavel!" It's hard to ignore a pink gavel.

Are your kids pounding their gavels for your attention?

Don't put off dating your kids any longer. At our house, Cheryll and I have learned that when we bring the groceries home, we must stand guard over the bags and eat anything that we really want right there and then. Once things disappear into cupboard or fridge, they are gone for good. Same with television. If there's a show you want to see, don't dare leave during a commercial—and always keep the remote control tucked firmly under your armpit. Doze off for even a moment, and you will be startled awake by a cold armpit and the sight

SAY, "WOULD YOU

GO ON A WALK

WITH ME?

I JUST WANT TO BE

ALONE WITH YOU

FOR A WHILE!"

of Mad Dog Donovan cannonballing into the stomach of Rabid Randy Rawlins.

Your kids need you now. If you're not there, they will change the channel. When you look around for them, they will have gone somewhere else for that kind of attention. And how will your children learn how to date people outside the family—and enjoy themselves without awkwardness—if you haven't modeled for them what a fun and memorable date is?

One way is to date your spouse often and in creative, inexpensive ways. We buy two-for-one coupon books and keep our eyes peeled for special deals. With a coupon off the back of a cereal box, we went for a bed-and-breakfast "two-fer." We chose a beautiful little inn on Whidbey Island and slept in the century-old bedroom of a sea captain. A gourmet breakfast featured hazelnut quiche and fresh raspberry parfaits. We bought perfume from Ireland, a tartan tie from Scotland, and loganberry syrup for the kids. Three days only, but they were a rich, restoring three days, personally selected with each other in mind.

TAKE YOUR CHILD OUT FOR A HOT FUDGE SUNDAE, OR ANY TREAT YOU BOTH LOVE. THEN SAY, "YOU KNOW WHAT? I LOVE YOU MORE THAN A MILLION HOT FUDGE SUNDAES!"

We also anticipate grocery shopping as an opportunity to snatch a few moments away and to favor each other with a maple bar or an ice-cream cone. The kids see that we treat even those more mundane moments as special opportunities to delight in one another as friends, making a routine task much more pleasurable.

Bless their little intrusive hearts, the children feel our friendship even when Mom and Dad are absent on a date of their own. That's because Mom starts looking for a phone booth before we've reached the city limits: "Do you suppose they're all right? Do you think they'll get along? Will they remember to feed the cat? Do they have enough lunch money/frozen dinners/deodorant/clean underwear to see them through?"

I love that woman. Perhaps that little prickly sensation at the back of her neck that something has to be amiss stems from two occasions in particular when we returned home to find that: a) one brother had attempted to drive the other's front teeth through the coffee table, and b) one sister had landed on one brother's index fingertip and snapped it. The latter occurred five minutes before I was supposed to take the broken boy to a music concert with his then-favorite a cappella group, *The Nylons*. Instead, he went to the emergency room and the date went to the younger brother.

But when the kids see their parents return from dates loaded down with trinkets for children, they are again reassured that as good friends, they are never very far from our thoughts. Whether it's a T-shirt from the beach, gift shop business cards for Nate's collection, or something as simple as motel soaps and shampoos, they know we went away because we needed some refreshment in our own husband-wife friendship, not because they drove us to it.

Such concentrated consideration came so naturally to me when my wife and I became engaged. Our courtship was a happy time of each trying to outdo the other in ways that personalized and made our relationship unique from all the millions of other man-woman pairings since creation. We spoke in a "sweet nothings" code with arched eyebrows and inside phrases that even the most determined of World War II decoders would have found impossible to crack. We wrote joyous, optimistic epistles of love that make us blush to read now. For each, the other was the only person on the face of the earth who could evoke such total, unquestioning enthusiasm.

The marriage bed needs such unbridled eagerness to please in order to flourish and blossom forth. The Bible clearly speaks on the strengthening power that this kind of undivided closeness brings to a partnership: **One standing alone can be attacked and defeated, but two can stand back-to-back and conquer** (Ecclesiastes 4:12 TLB). The last half of the verse shows that the assurance of victory is greater still when the partnership becomes a family team: . . . **three is even better, for a triple-braided cord is not easily broken.**

OUT OF THE BLUE, MAIL YOUR CHILD AN INVITATION TO ICE CREAM AND BOWLING OR POPCORN AND A VIDEO. KIDS LOVE MAIL, AND IT SHOWS THEM YOU THINK THEY ARE SPECIAL ALL THE TIME.

I must work to make my family team strong, unbreakable. To take them on customized dates of their devising is just one way. I like their choices. Shane used to be crazy for undersea life. He once chose a trip to the aquarium, complete with seafood snacks at dockside, accompanied by a magnificent sunset. Even our little guy at the age of two-and-a-half was dazzled by lunch in a restaurant where the waitress fussed over him and served his very own strawberry juice drink with red cherries skewered on a plastic sword. To this day he's nuts for maraschino cherries.

A trip to the barber with treats after, a walk and a picnic lunch beside the lake, putting a model together with pizza ordered in, or a scavenger hunt in the park may not be equivalent to Disney World, but they will be treasured and cherished for the rest of their lives.

Let them know ahead of time with an invitation sent through the mail. They love mail and the feeling of importance it brings. This

DO SOMETHING

"POSH" TOGETHER,

LIKE GO

TO A PLAY, HAVE

DESSERT IN A

FANCY RESTAU-

RANT, OR TEST

DRIVE A CADILLAC.

advance notice gives them opportunity to anticipate and plan, adding greatly to their excitement.

My kids like to bring their own allowance so they can contribute to the outing. It's especially fun for them to buy Dad a candy bar or a souvenir. One night one of my sons and I simply went to the rescue mission service and sang two hymns for the men gathered there. It was a memorable way to combine service with time alone.

You will make discoveries too, like how varied your children's interests, hopes, and dreams are. They often confide and share things on a one-on-one date they won't or can't divulge while having to compete for your attention at other times. I hand out a great deal more praise and far fewer reprimands when the challenge of integrating the six personalities of my combined family has been reduced to the intimate confidences of just two sharing a date.

A date with Dad. Why, I've even been known to enter a sack race with my kids, despite an inexplicable aversion to burlap.

Chapter 9

WEEPING, WAILING, AND GNASHING 101

If you're a business person, you've probably heard it said that it costs five to six times as much to attract a new customer as it does to keep an existing one, so take better care of the one you've got. I submit that the same is true of children.

There are days when we want to scrap the kids we've got—like when they bend over backwards to make time for and to please everyone else's parents, but when you ask them to take out the garbage they gag and say, "How come I always get stuck with all the dirty work around here?"

They call you at work to ask you to rush home and pick them up so they can be dropped off for their shift at the Snatch 'n' Go Drive-In, solemnly promising that they will be ready the instant you get there so you won't have to miss your appointment with the president. But when you arrive out of breath, just having taken your own life in your hands, they are still running around in their Fruit of the Looms demanding to know what you've done with their uniform.

They eat your food, hog your phone, deplete your toilet paper, soil your carpet, use your car, run up your light bill, and then declare, "This place is a jail!"

Get a grip. No matter how finicky or trying the kids you have, they are still cheaper at this stage than making new ones, borrowing someone else's, or adopting in the hope of getting a rocket scientist.

Whenever I start hyperventilating over the kids, I try to remember the sage advice of Slippery Sam the Used Car Man: "Don't think of that Buick as a twenty-five-hundred-dollar investment. Think of it as only twelve-and-a-half cents a pound. Even lemons don't come that cheap, and would I sell you a lemon? (Wink, wink.) For less than a cup of coffee, a pack of gum, or a ride on the merry-go-round, you can own a pound of car!" That's fine if you can squeeze into a one-pound Buick.

I figure our children have cost us about five hundred dollars a pound. I could have had a fleet of lime green Buicks by now.

Actually, it is good advice to focus on just one piece of the pie at a time. When I set out to write my first novel, the thought of filling 350 pages made me wobbly in the knees. But I had written lots of magazine articles that, when combined, consisted of more words than a single novel. So instead of thirty chapters, I began to think of the book as thirty articles. As soon as I finished one article, I would start on another. By the time I completed a score-and-a-half of articles, I'd have a book.

GRAB YOUR CHILD IN A BEAR HUG AND SAY, "YOU ARE A LIVING MIRACLE!"

So focus on one child at a time, one day at a time, and pretty soon you'll have an adult of your very own. Of course, by then *you'll* be jabbering like a baby, but at least it's not uncommon.

I think back to 1975 and our little five-pound preemie lying there so fragile and alone, her skin yellow with jaundice, her eyes taped shut with giant cotton balls against the glare of the life-giving hospital lights. Her weak, tiny little cries were at least a sign of life. Some of the neighboring plastic isolettes were all but silent.

There was no price in all the world I would not have paid to spare my little bitty baby the trouble she was in. But I look now at the marvelous young woman Amy has become and think what a great mother she will make. What wonderful compassion she has for little ones! We are convinced her nest will one day be full of youngsters of her own. Was it her newborn fight for breath and strength that formed such a tender heart?

We call Amy Renee our Roo, Me-Roo, Me, Aimwhy, Aims, Aimers, and Amy Girl. Seventeen years from a premature birth when she could barely be heard above the hum of medical equipment, she traveled to Europe with her high school jazz choir to make a joyful noise. Today at twenty-four, she has a bachelor's degree, a fine husband, and the same heart of gold.

Though she may have the most tender disposition, Amy shares a compassionate and sensitive spirit with her brothers and sister. They all laugh, cry, and sympathize with an ease that I believe comes from a tender upbringing. Because Cheryll and I were their friends, we taught them that weeping, caring, and feeling all spring not from weakness, but from strength of character.

They need to learn heartfelt compassion and tenderness from both father and mother. We've taught our sons, as well as our daughters, that honest tears and affection are marks of genuine friendship and creative genius. Charles Dickens wrote with great emotion and sensitivity. "Heaven knows we need never be ashamed of our tears," he said, "for they are rain upon the blinding dust of earth, overlying our hard hearts." He knew full well mankind's cruelty and sought by his work to rain humanity on the hearts of his readers.

We need literature that tugs at the heartstrings and exercises the gentler, more compassionate parts of a child. Such public servants as William Bennett know this, and publishers are bringing out books like Bennett's *The Book of Virtues* which are filled with stories that stimulate the best in a child's heart. *Lobo the Wolf, The Lost and Found Puppy,* and *Black Beauty* also qualify.

If we don't tenderize our kids when they are young, especially our boys, we will live to regret it. If we sow indifference and self-preservation by allowing the media and our society to train up our children, we will lose the kind of generation which demonstrated such self-sacrificial concern on the *Titanic*. If the *Titanic* went down today, would men give up lifeboat seats to women outside their immediate families or to children? Would they give up their lifeboat seats to their own wives?

God, of course, demonstrated the ultimate compassion for us. He did not summon us to heaven in order to explain what He is all about. He came to us in Jesus and modeled for His disciples (and for you and me) who He is and what it means to live an upright life. God became understandable in the daily routine of our lives.

All of us are preemies in the eyes of God. If He did not reach down and save us—as the doctors and nurses did for our little one, too weak to survive on her own—we would die in our sin and spiritual frailty.

A coworker of mine discovered this when she attempted to climb a very steep and dangerous hill. Halfway up, she felt herself slipping and knew that she would fall and die, or at the very least be seriously injured. She threw her hand out for the only thing near—a thorn

TODAY, SHOW

YOUR CHILDREN

WHAT IT MEANS

TO BE TENDER,

OPEN, AND

UNAFRAID

OF FAILURE.

bush. She grasped it for dear life, and though it tore her flesh, it held and stopped her plunge. It was her lifeline, and she would not have turned loose of that thorn bush for anything. Nor can we embrace Jesus Christ without grasping hold of the crown of thorns. Only the pain and suffering He endured can break our fall into utter darkness and death. The way of the Cross is not always pleasant, but it is the only way that leads to eternal life. Our children need to understand that.

Have we done for our children what God did for us? Have we taught them by our living example what it is to be a gentleman or a gracious woman? Please don't wait. Don't make them come to you. The world cries out for us to unleash our kind and caring kids to do battle against the forces that would suck society under. The FBI reports that violent crimes by juveniles have soared to an "unprecedented level" throughout the nation. We are experiencing more than just a few isolated incidences of kids killing kids in their schools, which was unheard of and unimaginable twenty years ago.

In my own backyard, one report revealed that a tougher, more violent breed of juvenile offender overwhelms the Washington state juvenile justice system and accounts for one-third of all violent crime arrests. This is despite the sweeping Juvenile Justice Act of 1977, which was supposed to increase the number of children rehabilitated from a life of delinquency. Some say on the contrary, the act coddles teens and preteens and effectively shuts parents out of the process altogether.

All the social experts can think to do is throw a fifty-million-dollar reform package at the problem—if there were fifty million dollars to spare. How absurd to think that money alone could save families disintegrating from alcoholism, parent and child substance abuse, lack of parent responsibility and parenting skills, and laws that merely slap a juvenile offender on the wrist. The biggest factor of all is the fact that we have raised a generation of Americans with little or no religious faith and values. On June 11, 1992, my son gave the closing prayer at his public high school's graduation ceremony. Thirteen days later, the United States Supreme Court declared what he had done unlawful—official prayer at public school graduation ceremonies was suddenly unconstitutional.

Juvenile upheaval is probably not much different where you live. A 1999 Gallup poll on the attitudes of teenagers reveals that many of them don't feel safe and want to take training to defend themselves:

> Half of teens say they receive "too little" respect from adults, and many feel that they are misunderstood. . . . One-third of teens cannot talk about "life with father." When asked what relatives live at home with them, although 91 percent say their mother, only 67 percent say their father.[2]

Hands-on parenting is a rare thing for many teens; but when it is present, it can make the upheaval something you go through together and can reduce a lot of the fear they experience on the way.

In the Kelly home, we have striven to create a family full of "softies," myself included. The kids feel deeply and care very much that we think highly of them. Together, our family has sponsored orphans, hosted a sailor overnight, welcomed Japanese exchange students, delivered Christmas presents to

HELP YOUR CHILDREN TO ANTICIPATE "HEAVENLY PRAISE DAY," WHEN THEY SHALL HEAR GOD THE FATHER SAY, "WELL DONE, GOOD AND FAITHFUL SERVANT!"

---

[2] George Gallup Jr., "Teens Often Live in a Climate of Fear, Uncertainty and Danger," (28 April 1999) *Gallup News Service*. Website. Accessed: 3 May 2000, *http://www.gallup.com/poll/releases/pr990427.asp*

the children of prisoners, and gone caroling in the county jail. The kids have delivered food baskets through their schools; and once we took flowers out on a dock, and the children gave them to a couple of crew members of a Japanese log ship. Amid much bowing and delighted gesturing, the kids learned another lesson in international compassion.

Once during the Persian Gulf War, we were having lunch in a pizza parlor. Shane overheard two women talking. One expressed deep concern for her son in combat. As we were leaving, Shane asked the lady if he could pray for her son, and he did so on the spot.

Amy befriended a crusty old gentleman while helping weed his yard with her youth group. He didn't care much for religious talk, but he was touched by the young people's attention. Amy called him back a few times just to let him know that she was praying for him and that he shouldn't resist God so hard.

Nate volunteered for vacation Bible school and let little kids crawl all over him. He worries when I'm down and works hard to jolly me back up.

Steph has a big heart for street kids and the homeless. In Honduras one summer, she comforted little children who were the victims of abuse. One Christmas she spent three days on the streets of Seattle with only two dollars in her pocket and one piece of identification. She slept in church basements, but spent her days going where the homeless go, doing what the homeless do, learning all she could about their specific needs. In that time she was propositioned by a pimp, sought shelter in doorways, and visited the rundown emergency center known to the homeless as "Hell Hotel."

One Sunday she went to minister to the kids in our town's juvenile detention center. They asked many questions, from "How

WEEPING, WAILING, AND GNASHING 101

can God hear me when I pray?" to "Why are there no official pictures of God?" Steph received a spiritual workout that day!

One New Year's Eve we decided as a family to help Steph run Operation Nightwatch, a mission that attempts to locate shelter for street people. Steph manned the phones, Amy served hot beverages, Cheryll handed out clothes, and the Kelly men talked with the guys lined up out front hoping for a warm place to sleep. Only six had to be turned away. They were given blankets, and before they left we lit sparklers and cheered in the New Year.

No, it's not always easy letting the kids follow their callings. We naturally want to protect them and never send them into danger. But you don't coddle a friend. You help that friend find what they were put here to do. Don't be afraid to find out what that may be. Just provide a safe haven where they can come if they need to find shelter, sanctuary, and sustenance with you.

We let our kids seek us out after we'd gone to bed. As often as not, that's where some of the more meaningful conversations occurred. It's a safe place hunkered down between Mom and Dad. Nothing can get you there.

One morning, about two o'clock, there came a rap at my bedroom door. Cheryll was away at a conference. Steph asked in a shaky voice if she could talk to me. Of course she could, and soon she was beside me. Sobs racked her body. Her boyfriend had ended their serious relationship that night, and she could not sleep.

I began to weep too because my child was devastated and I could feel the depth of her

SAY TO YOUR CHILD, "WILL YOU COME AND SNUGGLE WITH ME? I ALWAYS FEEL SO COMFORTED WHEN YOU'RE NEAR."

sorrow. I wept because two fine Christian young people had not been able to find a oneness in service to the Lord. It had seemed quite promising for a time, but God in His wisdom had other plans for them both.

We clung to each other there in the darkness, father and daughter linked by the unbreakable bonds of blood and faith. How often I have held my kids and cried—boys and girls both—over change, over sin, and over questions without answers. Why do people treat each other that way? What came over me? Where was God when that happened? Why must I grow up? When will the pressures be less so I can enjoy life again? Why do I keep doing that which I know is wrong? Why don't I love God more than I do?

Even our times of anger with one another have almost always ended in tears of healing and restoration. Our antagonism suffocates and dies when we embrace. Business experts will tell you that when you have corporate conflict, it is most quickly resolved by sitting next to, not across from, the person with whom you are at odds. The clear signal you send is, "I'm on your side. Though we don't agree on this particular issue, once its substance is long forgotten, you and I will still be on the same team."

Your honest tears as a parent take you off the pedestal and place you in the trenches where your kids are. Shoulder to shoulder you advance on the enemy. Trade prayer requests with them and let them know when you feel that you have failed. To hear you acknowledge your imperfections will help them cope with their own. Remind them that the surest way to avoid failure is to take no chances. But faith without risk is a pretty bland affair. Every lasting success, particularly in the lives of God's people, is the direct result of risks taken.

My family is my flock. If Jesus the Good Shepherd, and the epitome of manhood, leads His flock tenderly, I as a father can do no less for my children. In Isaiah 40:11, we see the amazing tenderness of Jesus: **He tends his flock like a shepherd: He gathers the lambs in his arms and carries them close to his heart; he gently leads those that have young.**

Do you carry your young close to your heart? If we had a nation of mothers and fathers who did, child abuse and the horrible toll it exacts would not exist. Our kids would feel clean and strong and able to make a difference for God and country.

TELL YOUR CHILD, "I HAVE SO MUCH FAITH IN YOU!"

It is not too late for us to show tenderness and humility towards our children. Would you deny your child a pint of your blood or one of your kidneys? Of course not. So let them taste the salt of your tears, and they will be tenderized by it.

I will never forget an Easter sunrise service our church held on the deck of a friend's house. We huddled about our steaming cups of coffee and hot cocoa, diamond glints of sun flashing through the trees. Shane, sixteen, began to sing the song, "Watch the Lamb." Its stirring words tell of Jesus' supreme sacrifice as the spotless Lamb of God. When Shane came to the crucifixion scene, he began to weep unashamedly at the agony his Savior experienced to set Shane free for all eternity. The remainder of the song was a struggle for our son so overcome by God's grace.

It was a struggle for the rest of us too, but for his mother and me it was a bittersweet prayer of gratitude from a child's heart that had been rendered compassionate by the greatest compassion of all.

Chapter 10

CAREER DAZE

My very first published article was "The Adventures of a Male Mom" in *Mothering* magazine (Father's Day issue). I wrote it in 1977 when "house husbands" were all the rage.

I was one—a house husband, Mr. Mom. I learned cooperation from *Sesame Street*, safety from *Mister Rogers*, and how to dress myself from *Captain Kangaroo*. Whether or not the kids learned anything, I can't say, but after six months of that, I was a new man. The Fortune 500 companies are missing the boat by bringing in all these high-priced gurus of industry to train their employees in what spells success and productivity. If they would just send their whole workforce home for a week to watch those three shows, their problems would be over.

Our kids were four, three, and two at the time, with Nate still just a twinkle in God's galaxy. The four of us spent lots of time at the zoo, the park, and downtown feeding the squirrel and pigeon hordes. Mom was a secretary at an irrigation pump manufacturer.

I excelled at changing diapers, wiping noses, and whistling the ditty that played *ad nauseum* on the wind-up Fisher-Price toy radio. If just once I could have gotten a ball game or the weather report on that thing, I would have been happier. You've got to hand it to Fisher-Price, though. They build one sturdy radio. A grown man can crank on the winder gizmo with all his might, and it still won't snap—trust me.

The thing is, the kids knew what I did all day. One sure way to distance yourself from your kids and make them feel more like passing acquaintances than friends is to leave them in the dark about what you do at work. Oh, you're a great one for keeping detailed track of what they do, but what you do, where you go, and how food so "magically" appears on the table night after night is your Great Secret and their Great Mystery.

Solve the mystery and let them in on the secret as soon as possible. They are never too young to appreciate the sweat and creativity you pour into your work or the grinding humdrum you may have to endure to make ends meet. Somehow, some way, we have made it a point to include the kids in almost every job either my wife or I have ever held. We let them know they were as welcome in our world as we were in theirs.

TAKE YOUR CHILDREN TO WORK AND SHOW THEM OFF TO YOUR BOSS AND COWORKERS. TREAT THEM TO LUNCH IN THE COMPANY LUNCHROOM. OVER THE INTERCOM, ANNOUNCE THE PRESENCE OF "VERY SPECIAL GUESTS."

They want to feel a part of what you do. Shut them out, intentionally or otherwise, and you will lose good friends.

When Nathan wasn't even head high to a doorknob, he was sweeping carpets and bussing tables at Bison Creek Pizza. I have the most vivid picture of him in a bib apron doubled in two so it wouldn't drag on the ground. The ties passed around his middle about four times before they could be knotted. He wore one of those white paper hats to keep his hair out of the food and ran one of those mechanical carpet sweepers back and forth to pick up pizza crumbs. He was so cute and efficient the customers wanted to take him home.

I worked there part-time and my family would come in to eat on Friday nights. Almost without exception, the kids would hop to and fill napkin dispensers or salt and pepper shakers to take the load off Dad.

When we worked for a private Canadian boys' school and lived in campus housing, the kids went with us everywhere on our appointed rounds. They shadowed Mom to the laundry room and dispensed clean clothes. They joined in banquet preparations and helped in the serving line. They came to the classroom on a few occasions and watched me teach. They accompanied me to the chicken barn to help feed the broilers and behead the fryers. When market day arrived, they donned rubber boots and helped catch the reluctant fowl and carry them to the waiting semi for shipment.

The school kennels raised sled dogs, and though the kids could barely see over a husky or a malamute, they loved to groom the canine coats and never ceased to be amazed by the husky trait of one blue eye and one brown.

Back in the States, while older kids were in school, Nathan, who was five then, came along on my interviews for the newspaper. I had embarked on a freelance writing career and supplied the local daily with a couple of features a week. I'd introduce Nate as my right-hand man, and he was treated royally. When I interviewed the owner of a teen nightclub, Nate was allowed all the free video games he could play. The eighty-year-old diaper service lady plied him with fresh homemade pie. The owner of the San Francisco Giants minor league baseball team gave him a bat.

As the kids grew older, Cheryll took them to her office at Women's Aglow Fellowship International. There, they stuffed envelopes and filed while Cheryll did her regular credit manager's job. They received spending money for a few summer hours of work and gained a much better appreciation for their mother's contribution to both her employer and the running of our household.

Several years ago, I took Shane with me to the Christian Writers of Idaho Conference. He sang for the banquet, and we had a blast swimming and lifting weights together. We were even reproved by the hotel manager once for a too noisy session of towel snapping. People remarked on how close we were and how much they enjoyed having his youthful spark at some of the sessions. The man taking authors' photos was so impressed with our friendship that he took our pictures in color—for free. We had one of us together blown up poster size for Shane's bedroom and my office wall.

Again, Shane was right beside me experiencing what I experience in my work (minus the towel snapping). He listened to my banquet address and heard other perspectives on the writing craft. Plus, he made some unforgettable memories, like locking himself out of the hotel room and scaling the outside of the building to the second floor where he entered through an unlocked glass door! Ask at the desk for another key? Are you kidding?

> AFTER MOWING THE LAWN, DOING YARDWORK, OR HELPING WITH HOUSE CLEANING, TOAST YOUR CHILD WITH ICE COLD CANS OF SODA. "HERE'S TO JIMMY, A REMARKABLY CREATIVE SON. HIS WILLINGNESS TO HELP KEEP OUR HOME RUNNING MAKES ME PROUD TO BE HIS MOM (OR DAD)!"

He'd learned only too well from his imaginative writer-father to take a more creative approach to life and its little lockouts. Two years later I took Nate to the same conference. He had a key of his own!

Two of the kids attended Seattle Pacific University where I am a publications specialist. They not only saw the work I do but experienced a direct benefit by enjoying the quality education I help promote. They sometimes stopped by the office between classes, we went to lunch together occasionally, and they commuted with me to their campus summer jobs.

My wife and I have even—gasp!—let the kids see our paycheck stubs. Then they can better understand just how far we have to juggle just so much income. Otherwise, in a child's mind, parental money is infinite in supply and instant in availability. My parents argued about finances constantly, and I could never figure out why. One reason for my confusion was that they never took me into their confidence or explained to me the size of the pie.

But my dad did take me to work at a chemical warehouse for a day, and his boss paid me five dollars to help clean up. Dad was a commercial artist before his eyes went bad, and he was forever creating board games and greeting cards. I sold his beautiful redwood signs door to door, and I'm sure that it was partly on the strength of his fabulous campaign posters that I was voted student body president of my high school.

When I freelanced from home, I think the kids sometimes thought I was a glorified typist (some editors agreed). But occasionally, I could flip open a magazine and show them an article with my name on it. More important to the juvenile psyche, however, I kept candy bars and other forbidden delights in the lower left-hand drawer of my desk. They loved to find me after school, throw their arms around my neck, ask how my day went, and inquire after the state of my health—and I theirs. The quite astounding thing was that no matter how I twisted, turned, hugged, or kissed them during this

WHATEVER IT IS

YOU DO, WHEN

CAREER DAYS

COME TO YOUR

LOCAL ELEMEN-

TARY SCHOOL,

JUMP AT THE

OPPORTUNITY TO

STRUT YOUR STUFF.

happy debriefing, their eyes remained riveted on the bottom left-hand drawer. NASA could not do a better job of locking onto the Space Shuttle in preparation for re-entry.

"Dad, we're havin' Career Days at school. Ya wanna come 'n' talk 'bout typin'?" That's as coherent as a nine-year-old gets when she's feeding on a Hershey's chocolate bar.

"Oh, well, it's very nice of you to ask, dear, but I need to take my typewriter in and have the keys buffed."

It's not that I didn't want to share the life of a storyteller with a bunch of lively fourth-graders, but I had these recurring nightmares of TV's Bob Newhart standing naked—figuratively speaking—before a class of moppets taught by his wife, Emily, talking about the psychologist's life. He bombed. Bombed big. His dry ramblings on Freud and Gestalt just didn't stack up against Larry's daddy's fireman's ax or Susie's mommy's black belt.

Somewhere between the Hershey's bar and a wad of *Double Bubble* gum—don't tell her mother—I said yes. Then came home the slip of paper stating the day and time of my presentation. *Lord, give me strength.* I was to follow a bone surgeon with a skeleton named Max.

I did not want to bomb, but a no-show would signal that we literary typists are reclusive and cowardly. Nonsense! I distinctly recall spending a day in my son's preschool class and returning home smelling of peanut butter and guinea pig droppings. And there was that time I took the Siamese cat for Steph's show-and-tell, and it clawed me to ribbons on the way home. But how can one top Tommy Stoner's dad's police service revolver?

When I arrived in class, fifty-nine of the fourth-graders (I had both classes) were mercifully at recess. The sixtieth was my daughter. She appeared nervous. "Sorry 'bout the smell," she said, wrinkling her nose at the musty, damp atmosphere. "Drains backed up yesterday. Had a flood. Puppet theater didn't make it." Indeed it hadn't. A sodden mass of cardboard and construction paper slouched shipwrecked in one corner. An ill omen. The corner opposite was empty. Is that where I would be tossed?

A bell signaled the end of recess. The first arrivals searched about me as if I were a couch with something hidden behind. "Where's E.T.?" they demanded of my daughter. "You said he was bringin' E.T.!" She looked bilious. I looked confused. "Couldn't tell 'em you were bringin' a typewriter!" she hissed at me fiercely.

Swell.

What I had said was that I was going to describe the different kinds of writing writers do: writing the screenplay for the movie *E.T.*, for example. I smiled winsomely at my accusers. "E.T. wanted to be here," I said jovially, "but he had to—

"—phone home," they finished for me, dispiritedly slumping into their seats.

This was one tough crowd.

Once all were assembled and I was introduced as "the writer man," I opened an oversized black garbage bag and began tossing out everyday specimens of the ancient writing art: bumper stickers, greeting cards, newspapers, food labels, cereal boxes, Ronald McDonald calendars, letters, Garfield books, magazines, posters—the printed paraphernalia of a society gone mad with the printed word.

I spoke to them of character and conflict. Their slouches straightened a bit, and their eyes lit up when I asked for those two vital ingredients in the story of *Star Wars*.

"Luke Skywalker has to overcome Darth Vader and the Evil Empire!" they shouted back.

"E.T.?" I asked, enjoying the feel of them eating out of my hand.

"E.T. has to get home!" they boomed as one, nudging one another in delight.

"The Dark Crystal?"

"The geldings must find the broken shard from the crystal and bring it back before evil overtakes the world!"

If this was writing, then writing was *fun*.

"Writing begins with an idea," I told them. "Where do ideas come from?" Conversations, we agreed, and in the mini dramas played out daily to and from school, on the bus, in the store, and at home.

I was cooking now. Without knowing it, my job seen through the eyes of children was taking on a whole new shine—for me. Their laughter and eagerness for ideas reminded me of why I had become a writer. It was a delicious stew of people, things, and thoughts. I'd lost sight of that more than once and in so doing had become a mere typist of hackneyed phrases and characters as shallow as rain on the pane.

Career Days was a much-needed shot in the arm. The elixir of enthusiasm was mine once again. Without the aid of ax or black belt or a skeleton named Max, I had those kids right where I wanted them. I had no need for props—I had their *minds*.

"Okay, everyone, now it's your turn!" A ripple of interest washed across the room and back. I handed them copies of an innocuous bit of writing I'd done about a giraffe named Geraldine and her inability to choose just the right necklace for the Golden Summer Jungle Party. The minutes were ticking away before her date arrived, and all the other animals made decidedly unhelpful remarks as they passed on their way to the festivities. At last, along comes ravishing Priscilla Peacock with the perfect solution: "Wear them all, honey; you've got the neck for it."

Sixty budding writers almost fell over themselves to be the first to come up with the ending, which I had deliberately left off of their copies.

"Give it a title, gang, and be creative. Anything would be better than mine. 'Geraldine's Necklace' is just too obvious and dull—"

"Hey! That's the title I put!" piped up Jesse Walters in the second row. You could see the anguish in his eyes. On the one hand, he'd come up with the exact title the author had; on the other, it was rejected as patent drivel.

"Great title!" I recovered, not wanting to step on any budding James Micheners or Taylor Caldwells. "Honest, succinct, economical!"

The bell rang for lunch before I could define succinct. Who cared? Everyone wanted to sit by me in the cafeteria. My daughter sat on one side, and Tommy Stoner won the draw for the other. He allowed as how being a writer was safer than being a cop. He said I could carry a service revolver in my mind, could have it popping off all through my manuscript, and never once get hurt. His dad had been wounded twice.

Someone, I think it was Jesse Walters, said the mushy spinach was "Yuck!"

"Come on, Jesse," I urged. "Let's try for a little more originality there. For this stuff, we need a title that sings!" We formed an impromptu literary committee and took suggestions. Carly Brower won hands down.

"Henceforth," I whispered so as not to arouse the cook's suspicions, "the spinach served in this cafeteria shall be known as Green Glop Surprise!" The resounding cheer greeting that pronouncement earned our table two demerits for the week.

My daughter walked me to the car. As I was getting in, she tugged on my sleeve, gave me a huge hug, and said, "Thanks, Dad. You were better'n a rickety ol' skeleton. When I get home, think you could teach me some more 'bout how to make my writin' sing?"

I nodded and kissed her on the head. Obviously, another job for Writer Man.

But, I digress. Back in those lazy days of '77, I was just a house husband with a family pass to the zoo and a passion for Sugar Smacks cereal. I recommend that every father find a block of time to spend every day, all day with his children. Let them see that for you, fathering/mothering/parenting is one of the absolute top priorities in your life—*ahead of career.* You can be replaced at work. You are irreplaceable at home.

CLIMB A TREE WITH YOUR CHILD, THEN SHOUT TO THE WORLD, "I HAVE THE MOST SPECTACULAR KID ON THE PLANET!"

Who else but Dad would set his diapered daughter in the shade of a spreading willow tree and stand there wondering why she was shrieking, only to discover she was atop a red ants' nest?

Who else but Dad would push his child "Higher, Daddy, higher!" on the swing and watch gape-mouthed as she lost her grip and went parachuting into a grim-faced woman's picnic lunch?

Who else but Dad would claim a little boy who collects scabs in a jar?

What father on a bad day would want to miss a pat on the shoulder from a little hand and the wise words, "It's okay, Dee Dee, Jesus still loves you." In fact, what I wouldn't give to be able to tune into a wind-up Fisher-Price radio about now.

Chapter 11

THE ALL-VOLUNTEER CHILDHOOD ARMY

"Your dad home? May I speak with him, please?"

He stood there on the porch one blustery fall day, one empty coat sleeve flapping in the breeze. Old, white-haired, and rough-skinned, the little man waited expectantly for my reply.

"Dad!" I shouted over my shoulder. "A, uh, Mr., uh—"

"Sawyer," provided the stranger.

"A Mr. Sawyer here to see you!"

Dad spoke a few words to the visitor, and together they went out into the yard. Through the window, I watched Dad point at various locations in the garden while the little man gesticulated vigorously with the stub of his amputated arm. There really wasn't enough gardening to require the man's help, but Dad sensed Mr. Sawyer's need to be needed.

Mr. Sawyer made a daily pilgrimage to our house. The nimble, one-armed man spading with a shovel tucked under his stump, using a leg for leverage, became a familiar sight in the months ahead. With garden tools tucked into every available spot on his person, he would push a gas mower up to our picket gate and busily set about putting the yard to rights, planting the garden, and killing the weeds. He never asked for money and staunchly refused offers of payment, even though his humble home, two doors away, attested to a meager pension.

Seemingly ignored by his own children, Mr. Sawyer took pleasure in leading a life of quiet servitude to those nearby. Allowed to help, his joy and loyalty were beautiful to see, but blind resentment and selfishness blurred my vision.

Mr. Sawyer had one annoying fault. To him, flowers and weeds grew from the same stalk. More than once, the compost pile was adorned with Mom's jumbo nasturtiums. One day I planted a fir seedling between two huge shrubs for a school project. *Surely it would be safe there,* or so I thought. Mr. Sawyer pushed the mower between the shrubs. Good-bye tree.

I was livid. This intruder had stolen my father's time away from me, taken jobs I could have done but never would, and now he had killed my tree. For days, I seethed. Still, Mr. Sawyer came to dig, mow, plant, water—and love. But I was spoiled, avoiding him more and appreciating him less.

Then came tragedy. Dad was diagnosed with cancer. That fall, I entered college and was able to visit only on weekends. Driving in on Friday evenings, I'd see Mr. Sawyer pruning the hedges. As I drove away every Sunday night, he'd give me a wave of his stump without missing a single clip. At the funeral, he stood uncomfortably in an ancient tweed suit, tears clouding his usually snappy blue eyes. Finally, my heart softened.

Mom offered to cook for my best friend and me at college, so we put the house up for sale. Mr. Sawyer worked as diligently as if we were staying, perhaps with a renewed sense of purpose—Dad was dead and only Mr. Sawyer could keep the yard and garden alive.

At last it was leaving time, and Mr. Sawyer stood at our old gate waving his stump in farewell, tears again clouding his eyes, reluctant as ever to leave what was now someone else's home.

A few weeks later, a letter arrived from Mr. Sawyer's son saying his father had died. Faced with another death, Mom started to cry. I walked numbly out onto the front porch of our new home. I searched the yard longingly for a one-armed man with a shovel that never quit spading. Every shovel of dirt he had turned had been a lesson in servanthood. A man of little means or status, his existence known to few, had used what he did possess for the good of others.

OUT OF THE CLEAR BLUE, SAY, "I'M SO FORTUNATE TO BE YOUR DAD (OR MOM)!"

And he'd done it literally single-handedly.

How do we model and encourage servanthood in our children? We start them young by demonstrating that we ourselves do not always count the cost. One of my favorite writers' workshops to conduct is one I call, "Giving Your Writing Away." What I have found is that some of the most satisfying and productive writing I have ever done has been done for free. Letters to the editor, for instance, get results. In reply to one that I wrote against abortion, a young woman answered that my argument helped her choose in favor of life. Another letter I wrote against all the gloomy talk in a recession year landed me a one-minute spot on television giving my opinion. Thus inspired by my efforts and results, my daughter wrote a letter decrying the chaining of dogs in the beds of moving pickup trucks. She still keeps a copy of the published letter in her scrapbook.

I've written auction copy for the Northwest Boychoir, promotional copy for the United Way's Volunteer Bank, and brochure copy for a community club. Church newsletters, letters of recommendation, letters to my kids on the mission field—these and more are ways for me to model a servant's heart.

Cheryll's mom spurred Stephanie on to service by offering to go halves in sponsorship of an orphan in India. With Grandma's help, Steph's tithe money went twice as far, and it gave the two of them something special to share. She wrote to the girl and followed her school career through the responses. Ever since, Steph has faithfully sent her tithe money to help the poor.

We have practiced two key principles concerning money from the kids' cradle days on up:

1. The moment they first receive cash gifts, we teach them about tithing, or the giving of one-tenth of their gross earnings back to the work of God. It is not an option but the base minimum, and it needs to come off the top. It is most natural, then, to include tithing of their time and talents as well as their income. God gave us all that we have and are, and we must withhold nothing from Him, neither ourselves nor our possessions. Tightfistedness should not become a problem.

2. Allowances must be kept *low* or soon everything kids do around the house will bear a price tag. Ours began at seventy-five cents a week and topped out at three dollars a week, even for teenagers. Regular chores are one thing, but they must see that the *spontaneous* contribution—without pay—is the one that best expresses one's gratitude for home and family.

To get your youngsters off on the right path, keep track of local volunteer opportunities in the newspaper and start them young. Steph's love of animals was perfect for a volunteer opening at the animal shelter. Over time, she fed, watered, and scooped up after the animals, made bedding for the cats, and even went on stray animal patrol with the dog catcher. A few years later, those were credentials enough to land her a volunteer position with a local veterinarian clinic. If not for the dander in cat fur, she might have pursued it further. Amy also worked at the animal shelter for a time and has a strong affinity for animals.

Shane's love of marine life landed him a junior naturalist's position with the Seattle Aquarium for a summer. He led tours and learned volumes about sea life from staff biologists. That experience and two years in the Northwest Boychoir gave him tremendous poise and stage presence.

One year, the phone rang. It was the dentist calling. But instead of wanting the kids' teeth, the receptionist wanted their backs. Because she and the doctor had been so impressed with the kids, their attitudes, and activities, she was offering them a job weeding, sweeping, and otherwise maintaining the office landscaping. Amy and Nate answered the call.

A REPUTATION FOR DILIGENCE AND GOOD WORK, CULTIVATED YOUNG, WILL OPEN DOORS FOR YOUR CHILDREN.

At the age of twelve, Shane was hired to repair vacuum cleaners because of a fine five-year volunteer record. He had two money market accounts by the age of fourteen, and I've never had any! And what valuable experience he gained in both small appliance maintenance and earning a wage.

Because they have rolled up their sleeves and jumped in early, our kids have learned the truth of this statement in the corporate newsletter, *Communications Briefings:* "Work hard, not solely because it will bring you rewards and promotions, but because it will give you the sense of being a competent person. Something corrosive happens to the souls of people who stop caring about the quality of their work and begin to go through the motions."[1]

A willing heart and a winning attitude eventually landed Amy a job as a dental office assistant at the tender age of sixteen. Because she had done so well on the outside of the building, she was asked (and paid) to clean instruments and keep the place shipshape on the inside.

National studies show that American teenagers volunteer at the same rate as adults but that more would volunteer *if asked.*

True parent friends will applaud children's efforts to give of themselves. Show plenty of admiration and appreciation, but also remember that service is its own reward. Our kids thrive on the certainty that to give away time and talent is to receive incredible blessing in return. Over time, they have jumped at opportunities to be peer advisors, teaching assistants, and camp counselors. Steph even tackled some especially challenging work at an Easter Seals camp for disabled children and a Volunteers of America camp for retarded adults. Once or twice a month, she spent her nights finding shelter for the homeless. She has since worked with street kids in Mexico City.

The night the entire family joined her on the streets in Seattle, we all learned about service in the process. Steph was reminded that her family is behind her 100 percent. It was reinforced for each child that a servant's heart is to be highly prized for a healthy, meaningful life. Stereotypes about all street people being drunks or dope pushers were dispelled. We met Alaskan fishermen, an auto mechanic from Zaire, and a dad and his son passing through on their way to California in search of work.

---

[1] Quote by Harold Kushner in the January 1992 issue of *Communications Briefings*, 700 Black Horse Pike, Ste. 110, Blackwood, NJ 08012. n.p.

Do I worry that my elder daughter ministers in some dark places or that some of the children appear to be led to a life of service in dangerous places abroad? I wouldn't be a dad if I didn't have second thoughts about my children going into the streets or to an unstable Central American nation. But God has marked them for life, and I would be no friend if I prevented them from what, with all its dangers, will be an incredibly fulfilling future.

To be a true friend to your children, establish a pattern of service in your family life. Both Cheryll and I have held a number of volunteer positions in the church and the community, and Cheryll is especially big-hearted about dropping everything to help someone in need. Once, we invited kids from the state church youth organization to sleep at our house during a convention and ended up with fourteen kids on floors and couches. There was just one death that weekend—the water heater. Most of our guests were girls, and the ensuing heating of water on the stove for hair washings was a raucous, but caring, experiment in community.

"It is the church in overalls . . . pouring in the healing ointment on the open sores of a great city," said Francis O. Peterson, founder of Union Gospel Missions.[2] That attitude expresses a way of life that I want for my kids. Be a friend to your children by helping them get the focus off themselves in order to find enjoyment in service to others.

How? How can you as a parent buck the self-centeredness of youth? Certainly by modeling selflessness. But it is more than that. You need to be shrewd in your approach. Don't hit them with, "Here's something I think you should do." Instead, relate a volunteer activity to their particular interests or career goals. Show them how

---

[2] Quoted from "More Than a Thousand Points of Light," by Herbert A. Pfiffner (Seattle, WA: Union Gospel Mission, 1992), p. 57.

SPONSOR AN

ORPHAN IN YOUR

CHILD'S NAME. SAY,

"BECAUSE YOU'RE

SUCH A BIG HELP

TO ME, I'D LIKE

YOU TO MEET

SOMEONE WHO

COULD SURE

USE YOUR

ENCOURAGEMENT."

valuable it is to develop a résumé of involvement that demonstrates a concern for others and the neighborhood or community. Scan local newspapers and bulletin boards or call specific agencies for volunteer needs. In some cities, the United Way maintains a volunteer computer database that lists the needs of the agencies United Way supports. Tell your kids what you've found out and offer to go with them the first few times. Or volunteer yourself and take them along. When our kids saw that we were willing to audition for a part in summer theater, their enthusiasm was sparked even more.

READ TO YOUR CHILDREN FROM BOOKS ON ABRAHAM LINCOLN, FLORENCE NIGHTINGALE, AND OTHER PRAISEWORTHY PEOPLE. WHEN THEY DO SOMETHING TO SERVE OTHERS, STOP AND TELL THEM HOW MUCH THAT ACTION REMINDED YOU OF SOMETHING ABE OR FLO WOULD HAVE DONE!

Don't worry if at first they seem less than excited. Once they experience the joys of service, you can soon back off if you wish, and they will take it from there.

My older son loves to sing and has a fine voice. He did at seven years of age. *What would happen*, I wondered, *if he were accepted into the Northwest Boychoir?* I showed him the announcement of auditions, and he thought it would be great fun to perform for audiences and go on tour. Well, he made it—the youngest ever accepted to that point—and sang for governors, performed in the Seattle Opera House, and gained entry to both malls and mansions. He has sung to orphans in Belize and opened professional sporting events with the national anthem. But by far his greatest discovery was how wonderful it is simply to put a song in the heart and a smile on the face of someone else. Today, he is studying for a master's degree in order to teach English literature.

One of my favorite examples of a life of service that paid incredible dividends is that of Saint Patrick. At the age of sixteen in Roman Britain, he lost his parents to marauders and was sold into slavery. He became a herder of cows and sheep in Ireland, a lonely occupation, but one that gave him plenty of time to pray and grow closer to God.

These were the Dark Ages, and the people all about him had embraced the Druid religion. They worshipped nature and offered human sacrifices to pagan gods. The Irish people were known as a happy and lovable lot, but they had chosen darkness. Patrick loved the country people and wanted them to know the love of the one true God.

For six years, he herded animals in solitude, forming a daily discipline of marking time by saying a hundred prayers each day and another hundred on the night shift. Then Patrick escaped and wandered in a wilderness for twenty-eight days.

Increasingly more determined to become a Christian missionary and return to help change the Irish people, he entered a monastery for four years in preparation for future service. After leaving the monastery, Patrick was captured by pirates but escaped to his family home where he spent the next *thirty years* studying the Scriptures in further preparation for a mission to Ireland. Finally, at the age of sixty, he felt ready to face the forces of evil!

With an entourage of coworkers who doubled as bodyguards, Patrick returned to Ireland and immediately encountered the terrible Druid priesthood and practitioners of sorcery. He waded right into the midst of their pagan festivals and declared the risen Christ. He traveled the land, encouraging peasants and priests alike to abandon the black arts.

Needless to say, Patrick was not popular among the Druids, and they tried numerous times to kill him. Though they attempted to burn him alive, the flames would not catch. They conspired to poison him, but he would not drink. Once they went after him with swords, but a wild storm broke upon them, and in the resulting gloom and confusion they killed each other with their own weapons!

Patrick's preaching turned hundreds of thousands of people to Christ. In a single day, twelve thousand conversions were reported. On Easter Day in A.D. 433, Patrick preached to a queen and her subjects about the Trinity. According to legend, because the concept was so difficult for them to grasp, he picked a three-leaf clover (shamrock) and showed them how it was three separate leaves, yet one stem. They were so astounded by the simple lesson from nature that the queen accepted Jesus on the spot, followed by the rest of her people. When royalty bowed the knee, everyone bowed the knee! In ten years, Ireland was transformed by the power of truth. Patrick, at seventy years of age, stood with the chief king of that island nation and heard him proclaim Christianity to be the law of the land.

> WHENEVER YOUR CHILD DOES SOMETHING NICE FOR SOMEONE, TELL THEM IT WAS A GODLY THING TO DO FOR **GOD IS LOVE** (1 JOHN 4:16) AND GOD IS PLEASED WITH THEM.

Patrick continued to travel the countryside, establishing many hundreds of churches and Christian schools. Because of the astonishing power of the Gospel of Jesus Christ delivered through this humble servant, it was inevitable that legends would spring up about Patrick. That he drove all the snakes from an island that never had snakes to begin with is one of the more famous. But Patrick knew better than anyone that he possessed no magical powers. His strength came entirely from God, and every waking moment for this tough but gentle man was another moment to work for the Lord.

That's what God can do with a giving, servant's heart. One of the friendliest things you can do for your kids, one that will keep them close to you in spirit for life, is to develop in them a Patrick-like simplicity and *availability* for whatever mission God has for them to undertake.

SAY, "YOU WERE SO KIND TOWARD THAT PERSON. DO YOU FEEL AS GOOD AS THEY DO?"

Tell them the story of Saint Patrick and teach them his song. "The Breastplate of Saint Patrick" is a prayer that he sang each day before heading out into the storm of ministry. Only too aware of the dangers and traps ahead, he made sure he began his day putting on the breastplate of God's protection.

"I bind myself today to the power of God to guide me, the might of God to uphold me, the wisdom of God to teach me," Patrick prayed. "Christ protect me today against poison, against burning, against drowning, against wound, that I may receive a multitude of rewards.

"Christ with me, Christ before me, Christ behind me, Christ within me, Christ beneath me, Christ above me, Christ at my right, Christ at my left, Christ in breadth, Christ in length, Christ in height. . . . Let thy salvation, O Lord, be ever with us."[3]

Go to the library, get the entire text, and make copies for your kids. Couple it with Psalm 46, which expresses much the same kind of assurance in God's help and which was often read by Martin Luther in times of trouble and danger. Read other biographies of

[3] Joseph Sanderson, D.D. LL.D. *The Story of Saint Patrick* (New York, NY: Wilbur N. Ketchum Publishing Co., 1902), pp. 263-265.

committed Christians to your children. Then send your children forth to serve with confidence. Risks faced in service to God are the only ones worth taking. Don't shield your kids from them. Friends challenge one another to servanthood and bask together in the many rewards of lives lived for others.

Chapter 12

YOU GAVE THEM BIRTH,
NOW GIVE THEM MIRTH

I stood in front of the Lola Hallowell Modeling Agency, smoothed my suit jacket, and read the sign in the window: "Professional talent and models for TV, films, radio, print work, and corporate videos. Men, women, and children of all ages. In business in Seattle since 1965."

It was just a small pre-midlife crisis. I was thirty-one. Nothing that a little "print work" couldn't fix.

In the waiting room I was surrounded by photos of two types: physically flawless twenty-somethings and older sea captains dripping with character. Square jaws and azure blue eyes, or full beards and weathered skin the texture of fine leather stared back at me.

Was there no place for plain, plump, and pasty?

It didn't matter. No sooner had my audience with Lola been announced, than I stood, and my zipper broke.

God, in His infinite mercy, had given me a briefcase with which to hide my shame. I affixed it firmly in front of me and took halting steps towards Lola's desk like a malfunctioning android. Lola is a small, compact, elegant woman. I felt as graceful as a three-legged musk ox.

I took my seat, and my fly split wide open.

Kind as Lola was, I know she had x-ray vision and could see through the briefcase. I was no model. I was a sweaty pile of dirty socks that had been delivered to the wrong building.

The interview must have lasted a week but ended finally. I debated whether to grip the arms of my chair and hump out of the room, or just wait until the janitor closed the office down. But it was obvious from Lola's expression that I was to stand and exit like a man. I stood and backed out of the room.

I know now how the party hostess feels when she first discovers that she has tucked her dress down the back of her pantyhose. There are no good parts for a man with a briefcase plastered to his fly.

Actually, I did land a bit part in a made-for-TV movie with actress Jill Ireland. They needed a furniture mover to haul one end of a sofa and say something like, "Where do ya want this, lady?" Alas, shooting was postponed and I was unable to reschedule. Just as well. I didn't own a pair of pants I could trust.

Tell stories on yourself (like this one), confide life's most embarrassing moments with them (like this one), and you take the sting out of your child's own adolescent awkwardness. When they see and hear you taking a relaxed attitude toward human foibles, they will lighten up and feel freer not only to "go with the flow" and "roll with the punches" but also to ride in your boat.

EASY, FREQUENT LAUGHTER BETWEEN PARENT AND CHILD IS ESSENTIAL FOR TIGHTENING THE BONDS OF FRIENDSHIP.

Speaking of boats, some of their favorite stories of mine involve the twenty-two-foot Indian freight canoes I used to steer on thousand mile, three-week wilderness journeys through the Canadian wilds. My crew consisted of high school boys from the private school where I taught, and my kids used to run along the banks of the Red River in Manitoba watching for their father's return.

As soon as we would touch shore, I'd go chasing my wife around in circles like some crazed bushman. "Voo-man! Beau-ti-ful voo-man!" I would growl, then pounce on one of the kids and hoist them on my back for a triumphant parade into the school dining hall where we voyagers would eat like there was no tomorrow.

But the stories of the trail were what they were after. They especially liked the one about the time our camp cook got the bags of orange powder mixed up and we starving paddlers dove into steaming hot cups of macaroni and butter-scotch pudding.

Their number one requested story, however, is rather delicate in nature. I tell it only by way of illustrating that it is the times when our human pride takes a beating that prove the most reassuring to others.

GET SILLY TOGETHER BY ACTING OUT DR. SEUSS, RECITING TONGUE-TWISTERS, OR HAVING A STARING CONTEST.

We wilderness canoers were a rough lot. We would cook in galvanized buckets over an open fire and sleep on the ground—no baths, toothpaste, or change of clothes to speak of. And for ease of access, we would each carry a plastic cup and metal spoon through the belt loop, connected by a length of heavy twine. That single cup was each man's dinner plate and drinking glass all in one. It was important that it be kept close and kept clean.

On one memorable trip I was expedition leader and, as was my habit, I would awaken a full half-hour before the rest of the camp, start the fire, and take a morning constitutional. Our latrine was essentially anywhere in the woods away from the main camp traffic.

This misty morning, I was still pretty bleary-eyed from a heavy sleep when I stumbled out to answer the call of nature. I found a suitable spot in the bush, squatted down, and neatly defecated into my cup.

SAY TO YOUR CHILD, "YOU'RE SO MUCH FUN TO BE WITH. LET'S PLAY!"

The mental picture of their father frantically scrubbing his dinner cup with sand every time the canoe put ashore for the next three days leaves my kids sputtering and gasping for air every time.

Dogs have been another source of bittersweet amusement. My fisherman son, Nate, loves hearing about the time I went salmon fishing on the Columbia River and caught my dog. For that particular species of salmon under those special conditions, I always used big silver lures with treble hooks on either end. When I went to cast, I always looked back first and yelled at Benny, my black-and-white beagle-terrier, to stay away.

On about the sixth cast, I again looked back to be sure Benny wasn't sniffing the lure. Between the time I looked back and then forward to cast, Benny stuck his nose on the lure.

I felt a gigantic tug on the line—the only one that day as it turned out—and then there began an ear-splitting yelping. I'd hooked my own dog through his right nostril.

Another fisherman held Benny down, and I cut the lure free from the line. Not a good idea. No sooner had I done that than my poor pooch whipped his head and hooked me through the knuckle of my right index finger with the one remaining free treble hook.

Master and dog, bound together by a salmon lure, were not happy campers. Benny tugged one way, I the other. I panicked and ripped the hook out of my finger with my left hand. The other fishermen helped bloody me get bloody Benny into the car, and I drove to the vet's, trying to keep the poor mutt still. The way he was shaking his head, I thought he would snag his eye for sure.

At the vet's, Benny lay on one table and I on another as the good doctor, tufts of cat fur clinging to his sleeves, patched us both.

Some years later, just before Cheryll and I married, she acquired a mongrel that was one part black lab and one part dachshund and looked like a seal. She named it Pudgy.

From the word go it was a one-woman dog that felt its sole duty in life was to keep me away from its mistress. That's a tall order for newlyweds. Eventually, Pudgy met his demise by eating bad fish. I swear I had nothing to do with it.

There are several other things about me my children find highly amusing:

- That I once played in the world's largest accordion band and that our selection for a command performance at California's Long Beach Civic Auditorium was the venerable oriental classic, "Yokohama Ferry Boat."

- That I suffered nicotine poisoning by chomping on an unlit cigar while playing a mobster in a modernized remake of *A Christmas Carol.*

- That at moments of stress I utter the same cornball and meaningless phrases my dad did like, "For crying in the sink!"

- That I worked as a reporter for an editor who held the two-fingered typing speed record, and who once threw a typewriter out of a second-story window in a fit of anger.

- That I interviewed a self-proclaimed religious guru named Man/Woman.

- That I published an article about rats that could gnaw through lead pipes and survive a fall from a five-story building.

- That I know a missionary to Africa who lost the forward gears in his van and drove 120 miles in reverse to make his village rounds.

- That my wife and I dance the polka; that when in a very light mood I will dance the Teaberry Shuffle; and that when in just about any mood I will do the Penguin Slide and make a face like a prairie dog.

These are important things to know about your father.

A sense of humor shows, among other things, that you have a healthy perspective on life and if, with all the responsibilities you have, you can laugh and enjoy yourself, your kids will more than likely develop a jolly outlook too.

Of course, humor doesn't come easily to everyone. For some, it is forced and doesn't happen naturally. To help keep my humor pump primed, I am a card-carrying member of the Fellowship of Merry Christians (FMC), an organization of ten thousand plus Christians of all denominations who love Jesus and love a good joke.

One of my co-clowns in the group is Tom Mullen, former dean of the Earlham School of Religion. This theological scholar travels around cracking jokes and helping folks heal through laughter. He says something especially profound: Laughter can help people

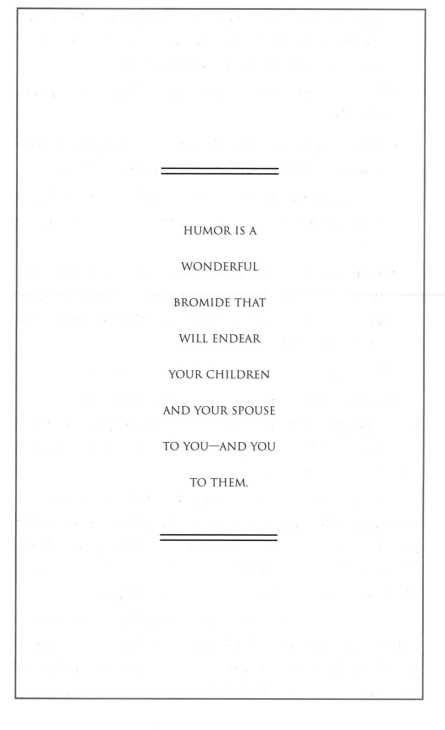

HUMOR IS A

WONDERFUL

BROMIDE THAT

WILL ENDEAR

YOUR CHILDREN

AND YOUR SPOUSE

TO YOU—AND YOU

TO THEM.

demonstrate their faith in God. If people can laugh in the face of adversity, it shows they believe that God is still in control.

Tom even pokes fun at his own diabetes. "I am a diabetic," he said in a speech at George Fox College in Oregon. "And if you want an illness that you can use to dominate table conversation, sugar diabetes is one of the best ones to have. You go in and have a meal and you don't eat dessert and someone says to you, 'Oh, are you on a diet?' and I say, 'No, my pancreas doesn't work.' And then I can elaborate on that and talk about my illness, and I'm the center of attention. I've talked about my pancreas much more since it stopped working than I ever did when it was working."

RECORD YOUR CHILD'S LAUGHTER AND PLAY IT BACK ONCE IN A WHILE. SAY, "NOW THAT'S MUSIC TO MY EARS!"

A father of four, Tom Mullen believes the power of humor is one of the most dynamic and potent weapons for any parent to wield. He feels that too often what we fuss at our children over are issues of little cosmic significance. The clothes they wear, the haircuts they get, and the state of their bedrooms are not necessarily issues where a life-or-death stand needs to be taken. If we are able to place these more "negotiable" areas in a humorous light, they will lose their overblown importance both to us and our kids. With all the biting, sarcastic humor they hear on television, how are they to know what is truly funny and does not ridicule others unless they hear and see it in action at home?

Humor in the home must be cultivated if you want your kids to want to come home. One of the nicest things about friends is how easily we can laugh together. Is yours a house of laughter?

Ten times a year the FMC publishes *The Joyful Noiseletter*, a six-page source of wholesome humor, jokes, and articles on humor and faith whose stated aim is to "recapture the spirit of joy, humor, unity, and healing power of the early Christians. We try to be merry more than twice a year."[1]

Some of the best lines on kids and family you'll find are those uttered by famous folk like Mark Twain: "Adam and Eve had many advantages, but the principle one was that they escaped teething." And your kids will appreciate this whimsical truth from Will Rogers: "An onion makes people cry, but there has never been a vegetable invented to make them laugh."

My mother taught me to laugh early and often. Hers was a hard upbringing on a farm in rural Washington, but even when her brother almost severed her toe with a hoe, she recalls dissolving in helpless laughter at his anxious cries of, "Mousey, mousey, up your blousey!"

Our kids have great laughs that I love to hear. Amy's probably takes the prize for most total involvement of every body part. Get her going, and it sounds like a cross between a chicken laying an egg and a Boeing 747 lifting off.

And I shall never forget the Saturday morning years ago when she and her siblings came flying into bed with Mom and me. We tickled and wrestled until Shane grabbed my feet through the covers and excitedly declared, "I've got Daddy's feet!" Amy sat up, looked singularly unimpressed, tossed her fair tresses, batted her lashes like a

---

[1] Write for details: Fellowship of Merry Christians, P. O. Box 895, Portage, MI 49081-0895, call toll-free 800-877-2757, or visit their webpage at www.joyfulnoiseletter.com. With your subscription, you will also receive a free humor book and access to a catalog of funny stuff, including lots of good family laughs with titles like *Happiness Is an Inside Job, I Was Afraid I'd Lose My Soul to a Chocolate Malt, Where Two or Three Are Gathered Together, Someone Spills the Milk, Life Everlaughter,* and *Peanut Butter Families Stick Together.* Plus much more about clown ministries, the humor of Jesus, and a treasury of cartoon books and funny cassette tapes.

famous beauty queen, and proudly proclaimed, "Big deal. I've got Mommy's eyes!"

A much bigger Shane landed on my bed one morning at 6:00 A.M. My wake-up caller had sopping wet hair from the shower and was only too happy to share it with me. Then he bounded to his feet and started flipping the bedroom light on and off. "Cool, strobe lights!" he chortled gleefully. I chucked pillows at him. "Ooh, 3-D!" he quipped, vanishing just as a size-eleven wingtip came sailing his way.

I remember little Steph getting bounced around on a skittish horse one summer. That ornery steed gave her a bumpy ride and refused to stay on the trail. By the time we stopped for a rest, Steph looked hot, rumpled, and grumpy. "How did Mary do it?" she demanded indignantly. We must have looked momentarily puzzled, so she explained. "I mean, how did she ever ride a donkey in her condition?" Good question.

Your teenagers may be a tougher audience for your attempts at levity. Where your eight-year-old loved your corny jokes and awful puns, your sixteen-year-old will give you one of those "Can we get real?" looks.

LET YOUR CHILD CHOOSE PAINT FOR THEIR ROOM IN ANY COLOR COMBINATION THEY WISH.

In the never-ending struggle to jolly up one's teenagers, I am encouraged by the humorous but practical approach some 7-Eleven stores took to discourage loitering by teens.

- They installed bright halogen lamps which made everyone look like zombies warmed over. Who'd want to be seen in *that* light?

- They switched to pointed garbage-can lids to prevent people from sitting on them. The teens soon got the point.

- They played elevator music in the stores. Like, gag me with a Barry Manilow LP.

Here are some ways to promote family fun and good humor after your kids reach thirteen years of age:

- Take them to see funny people with a point, like Messianic Jewish comedian Burt Rosenburg, or to a lively, upbeat, smileful performance of *Godspell* or *Cotton Patch Gospel*. Our kids enjoy Victor Borge, even though he's from another era. Quality humor is universal and spans any age.

- Take in a live performance of Theatre sports, audience participation, extemporaneous comedy clubs that prohibit offensive material.

> SAY TO YOUR CHILD,
> "IF YOUR SMILES
> WERE GOLD, WE'D
> BE BILLIONAIRES!"

- Attend a lively praise and worship time at a growing local church with your child. The jubilant songs and happy participants are infectious.

- Go camping whether or not you know a tent stake from an ice chest. The combination of water, fresh air, and "roughing it" makes for hearty appetites and light spirits. My boys just about coughed up a lung when I reached my hand into a bag of peanut candies left by the tent door, ate a few, and then discovered that a chipmunk had been ahead of me in line. He had done his business in the bag that I was left holding.

- Play Pictionary or a similar kind of timed team game with your kids. The action is so rapid it guarantees laughter and excitement.

Whatever you do, laugh it up around your house and show the kids the right way to make merry. Some wag even came up with a new beatitude for funny business. "Blessed is he who laughs, for he shall have company." Ben Franklin put a nice spin on it when he said, "Trouble knocked at the door but, hearing laughter, hurried away."

Homespun humor has one other important benefit—you can gross out your kids. On those canoe expeditions, I recall one particularly weird campfire on a tiny chip of an island in the Winnipeg River. It was pitch dark, bonfire flames leaping high, and pots of hot chocolate ready for drinking, when up from the ground rose hatching mayflies by the thousands. Into the fire they flew and down into our hot chocolate they fell. But after two weeks of hard paddling, you don't care if there are caterpillars doing the backstroke in there. "Drink up, me hearties, and don't mind the lumps. Protein, boys, protein!"

A story like that will send your daughters screaming from the room. Guaranteed.

Chapter 13

IN SEARCH OF THE JILLY KONG

I once had a dream about a Chinese restaurant called the Jilly Kong. It was so vivid, so specific, and so actual that the very next day I set out to live it.

It happened this way. My boss and I were staying in the San Francisco Bay Area on assignment for a chemical manufacturer. As public relations officers, our task was to monitor the pickets protesting outside one of the company's several plants. The pickets had grown belligerent in recent days and were strewing nails in the roadway and making threats against the truck drivers attempting to haul product out of the plant. We were to videotape the actions of the strikers in case of any future litigation.

Those were trying days. I felt none too secure in the little observation tower where the camera was trained on a number of unhappy and very burly men. They made obscene gestures, flashed large mirrors in my eyes, and made it quite clear what they thought of the company spy.

My boss was good company, and in the evenings we would take turns choosing restaurants. On one of my picks, I declared without hesitation, "Let's go to the Jilly Kong. It looks like it might have good food." A native of the area, he'd never heard of it, but I assured him it was not far from our motel. I drove to the "exact" location only to find a laundromat and dry cleaners instead.

I was unnerved. To so utterly believe in the reality of something that does not exist rattles the psyche and unsettles the soul. I could "see" the fuschias and greens of the neon sign with the little dancing Chinese characters. I could "feel" the cool, maroon Naugahyde of the eating booths. I could "taste" the fried rice with the tiny shrimp bits so carefully prepared by the dream cooks of the Jilly Kong.

We circled a few of the adjacent blocks in case I was a little off in my directions. But with mounting embarrassment, I finally had to admit that I had quite unwittingly made it all up. There was no Jilly Kong Restaurant.

We settled for a real Denny's.

PERIODICALLY HAVE A CANDLELIGHT DINNER WITH YOUR FAMILY. USE THAT OPPORTUNITY TO LET THEM KNOW HOW SPECIAL THEY ARE TO YOU AND TO GOD.

It was days before I could shake the eeriness of having been so completely fooled. My bogus restaurant was a fabrication of my subconscious. Although it looked like the real thing in my dreams, it was, in fact, all smoke and mirrors. I had believed in an illusion.

We fail as friends to our children when we leave their spiritual development to chance. When parents do not take moral and spiritual leadership in the family, kids will make up something to fill the vacuum, something every bit as "real" to them as my Chinese restaurant. What sadder sight is there than beautiful, healthy, God-breathed young persons devoting their lives to hedonism or some guru, shaman, or trendy psycho-babbler, because moms and dads did not lead? In all sincerity perhaps, they believed they were doing their kids a favor by letting them choose their own "religion." What they were doing instead was making their kids easy pickings for evil.

We do it in the name of toleration. A kind of cult of tolerance has risen in America where we become so open-minded our brains fall out. The truth is, if we do not provide spiritual light for our children, they will fall and hurt themselves. As my pastor said recently, you don't hike on a mountain or pick blackberries in the dark. He once declared that there would be no lights on a camping trip with his family. No flashlights, no lanterns, no campfire because any one of those things would disturb the pristine night and mask the awesomeness of the stars.

Three things caused him to regret his ban on lights:

1. Setting up camp in the dark.

2. Lying on a bed of pointed sticks and jagged rocks all night.

3. Settling down in the basin in which he'd erected the tent sight unseen. When the rain began, the basin filled.

If only they'd had a light.

Parents must show their children what God is like and what His expectations are, or sons and daughters will pitch their tents in wet places and spend their lives searching for a Jilly Kong that is not there.

Moses must have wondered at the Israelites' habit of checking their brains at the door. They not only left their flashlights in Egypt, they worked hard to quench the exceedingly bright pillar of fire God used to lead them by night. And how many of us leave the "flashlight" of God's Word, the Bible, unused in a drawer?

According to *Discovery Science Center*, "The numbers of possible combinations of synaptic connections among neurons in a single human brain is larger than that total number of atomic particles that make up the known universe."[1] You'd think with that kind of sophisticated equipment we'd have the intelligence to know that without a guiding light, a child will fall in darkness. You'd think we could remember to turn off the stove or put out the slug bait. You'd think.

MAKE YOUR CHILDREN'S SPIRITUAL DEVELOPMENT AN ABSOLUTE TOP PRIORITY.

As the leaders of our family, Cheryll and I light the way for our kids. We do that in a variety of ways, including not leaving their faith, their belief in and commitment to, their Maker to chance.

Warren Bennis writes in his book, *On Becoming a Leader,*[2] that all effective leaders, parents included, share certain ingredients. Among them are these paraphrased traits:

1.   *A Guiding Vision.* They have a plan, are dedicated to it, and inspire others to embrace it as well.

2. *Ability to See the Long View.* They are able not only to follow a plan, but to articulate the destination and how to get there patiently.

3. *A Passion for the Job.* They demonstrate a love for the work and the workers.

4. *Curiosity and Daring.* By their very zest for life and intense interest in it and how it works, they compel others to live it to the fullest. They see adversity as a teaching tool.

5. *Optimism, Faith, and Hope.*

The last set of ingredients—optimism, faith, and hope—are especially important in helping children develop a resilient outlook

---

[1] "Brain Facts," *Discovery Science Center.* Webpage. Accessed 4 April 2000. http://www.go2dsc.org/brainfacts.htm

[2] From *On Becoming A Leader* by Warren Bennis. Copyright © 1989, 1994 by Warren Bennis, Inc. Reprinted by permission of Perseus Books Publishers, a member of Perseus Books, L.L.C. pp. 39-41.

ATTACH AN

ENVELOPE TO

THE OUTSIDE

OF YOUR CHILD'S

BEDROOM DOOR.

MARK IT "PRAISE-

O-GRAMS" AND

PERIODICALLY

"MAIL" THEM

A NOTE OF

ENCOURAGEMENT.

on life and a "game plan" for reaching their goals. One of our kids, out of the depths of despair in a particularly stressful school year, said, "I can sure see what could drive some people to suicide." On another occasion when the parent-child bonds were undergoing rapid change and strain, this same child cried, "This is the kind of thing that sure makes a person think about running away!"

I felt like running away too and told him so. It was about this same time that I came as close as I've ever come to slugging my son in anger. My fist was clenched, my arm was cocked, my body felt cold. I shoved him hard but the blow never fell, and for that I'm grateful. Soon afterward, he and I went out to enjoy some special time, just the two of us, and today we love each other with a strong and binding love that thankfully transcends the tug and pull of growing up.

It is in those sometimes gloomy teen years that we desperately need optimism, faith, and hope, rooted in spiritual conviction. During those times of intense struggle, my son felt pretty pessimistic, but because Christianity is grounded in optimism, he fought mightily against the flood of negativity that so easily erodes a person's esteem and stymies his forward drive. A depressed child of God sounds like a contradiction in terms, but Moses, King David, Job, and Saint Paul all experienced their own private hell. Jesus was so distressed over His impending death and the sins of the world that He wept and sweat **as it were great drops of blood falling down to the ground** (Luke 22:44 KJV).

That is why, as leaders and friends to our children, we must build their optimism, feed their faith, and fan their hope.

The first time my little boys or little girls tried to walk, the attempt was an utter failure. But after the initial shock of landing with a bump, a sweetwise (opposite of streetwise) tiny smile would overtake the fallen one, and up the kid would come for another attempt. Did I say, "What an idiotic thing to try! The very idea that a wobbly thing like you could walk. Preposterous!"? No. I smiled radiantly at the thought that my little man or little woman was hitting the big time. Walking! Wow! Imagine that! "Good job, you little rug rat," I clucked. "Go ahead. Give it another shot!" My whole being said to that child, "Honey, you're going places, and I'm right behind you all the way!"

The only thing that gets a bigger rise out of a parent is the first day their precocious toddler uses the potty on their own—yet not without mishaps and relapses!

Do you recall the first time you went swimming as a kid—and sank like a rock? Do you remember your first time at bat, when you struck out? What about your first day on the job when you broke six glasses? Those were all failures, but did they make you stop swimming, stop playing ball, or stop working? Optimism made you come back for more.

God dusts us off after every fall and says, "See that glow on the horizon? That's home, that's the heavenly city. You'll be safe, warm, and welcome for eternity there. Run along now, stay on the path, follow the lights, and we'll make this run to Glory together!"

> PRACTICE OPTIMISM. A SUNNY DISPOSITION LETS YOUR CHILD KNOW YOU ENJOY THEIR COMPANY. WATCH THEIR SELF-CONFIDENCE GROW!

That's what we need to tell our kids. "Fail smart, kids. Learn and move on." Even in football, another chance to score is called a "down." We must never lead our children to believe that a winning, optimistic lifestyle is of their own making. Our final success or failure is based on obedience to God, especially in believing or rejecting His

Son, our Savior, Jesus Christ. Their success is ensured by their devotion to Him.

Deuteronomy 27 is a chapter of the Bible devoted to what occurs if you live a life of disobedience. In it is a litany of spiritual failure and the cursed results, from idolatry and sexual immorality to murder and bribery. But wait. Chapter 28 immediately follows: a wonderful affirmation of the incredible success enjoyed by living a life of obedience to God. Among other things, you will be blessed with an abundance of crops, livestock, and babies! Enemies will be defeated, rain will be abundant, and nations will respect you. You will be the head, not the tail; on top, never on the bottom. (See Deuteronomy 28:1-13.)

If we fail to put the preservative salt of God's truth in our kids, they will rot like unpreserved meat and fall prey to the sins and consequences of disobedience. The best homework assignment I ever had was the time my science teacher told me to place a chunk of raw hamburger under the front porch. The flies came, laid their eggs, and before long I had the neatest batch of maggots on the block.

But how terrible if I leave my children to the maggots. Unattended, left to their own devices spiritually, they will breed that which destroys. In those years when I bear tremendous influence over them, I am given awesome power and responsibility to quite literally make or break them. If I do what is morally right, they will follow suit. If I say what is morally right and wrong, they will develop a similar understanding. If I fight for truth, they will join the battle. If I demonstrate, as Jesus did, a love and concern for people and their problems

PRAISE YOUR CHILD FOR DOING SOMETHING KIND FOR A FRIEND. SAY, "IN A WORLD FULL OF SELFISH PEOPLE, I'M PLEASED TO KNOW SOMEONE AS THOUGHTFUL AS YOU!"

regardless of their race, sex, creed, or political persuasion, my kids will treat others likewise. If I model excellence and integrity in my work and in all my dealings with others, my children will strive for quality in all they say and do.

Above all, we must unblinkingly challenge our children with the claims of Jesus. An attempt one spring to do that in public caused an uproar in a small community near us. Spectators at a Norwegian parade were startled by an unexpected sight. A man dressed as Jesus and covered in blood dragged a cross, while a man dressed as a Roman centurion violently whipped him.

Obviously, this was not the usual happy-go-lucky parade!

Kids were reported to have been terrified, and outraged parents complained to parade organizers that their children suffered nightmares. Moreover, the reaction of the crowd was very diverse. While one boy desperately attempted to stop the beating of Jesus, other boys were yelling to strike harder.

Though many found the Jesus entry to be offensive, some members of the church that sponsored it thought the parade beer truck and the belly-dancers were more offensive. They expected people to be shocked, but their thinking was that the reality of the price Jesus paid for our salvation would also be pwerfully portrayed. And in this graphic portrayal, people would find hope by seeing how deeply God loves them.

I don't know how appropriate the graphic Jesus entry was to a patriotic parade celebrating Norway's independence, but I am struck at the parallels between the scene described above and the actual events of Jesus' journey to the cross. The Gospel, by its very nature, is an offense to the unbeliever. Can it be that there is any occasion where the Gospel is inappropriate?

Regardless, in our homes Jesus should be the natural daily rule, not the occasional offensive exception. Why would parents pass up or turn down the things God promises to them and their children? In Psalm 40, David acknowledges the Lord's rescue.

I waited patiently for the LORD; he turned to me and heard my cry.
He lifted me out of the slimy pit, out of the mud and mire; he set
my feet on a rock and gave me a firm place to stand.
He put a new song in my mouth, a hymn of praise to our God.
—Psalm 40:1-3

Romans 1:16 promises the **salvation of everyone who believes,** and in Philippians 4:19 the apostle Paul assures his readers in the church at Philippi that **God will meet all your needs according to his glorious riches in Christ Jesus.** Rescue! Salvation! Riches! What can you do, buy, or say that would come anywhere near producing those kinds of benefits for your sons and daughters?

Our friend, Susan Blakely, became pregnant for the first time. Being a media affairs person, she and her husband, Neal, wanted a birth announcement for the blessed event that was fun and unique, but one that the child could one day read and clearly understand their place in the divine plan. This is the resulting "Press Release":

Blakely, Inc. to Launch New Product June 1991. Seattle, Wash.—Blakely, Inc., a corporation with operations in Seattle, Fort Worth, Texas, and Missoula, Montana (grandparents), announces the launch of its new product, Baby X.

"This product will be a scaled down version of our former models," says Susan Blakely, spokesperson for the company. "We expect it to be available for viewing in mid-June."

To date, the product will be called 'Baby X.' However, two prototypes have been suggested, i.e., Travis Van and Sara Elizabeth.

Neal Blakely, president and CEO, shared his plans for the new product. "Our hope is that the product will function at optimal efficiency, and have a propensity for mountain climbing, fishing, and piano."

He adds: "This product should appeal to a wide market segment. Anyone wishing to obtain a copy of the construction plans should read Psalm 139:13-16."

Sara Elizabeth, the prototype that eventually emerged, will one day turn to that Psalm and read that she was fashioned in her mother's womb, **fearfully and wonderfully made** (Psalm 139:14), and that all the days of her life were ordained and written in God's book **before one of them came to be** (Psalm 139:16).

What a tremendous start for that child! What a legacy to be told that she was no accident and that everything in her life from the moment of conception is orchestrated and nurtured by the Supreme Creator.

Tell your children they were meant to be and that from day one they have a purpose and destiny that, if they eagerly seek, they shall find. It matters not if they were a "surprise" or born out of wedlock, they are here and they are known by God, the one who gave them life. Then you can rest assured that they will be less likely to search to and fro for the Jilly Kong that is not there.

Chapter 14

CARS AND OTHER FIENDISH INVENTIONS

Someone please tell me, what earthly good are cars? Other than providing a soundproof place for teens to talk where their parents can't hear them, what purpose do they serve? They consume your money and time, pollute the air, crash, and break down at the most inconvenient times. They take your wallet and wring it dry. They scratch, dent, get dirty, and malfunction with alarming regularity. They steal your exercise and add fatty deposits around your heart, a battleship around your hips, and a noose around your neck.

Who invented them anyway? Insurance companies? Auto clubs? Ronald McDonald? Certainly not anyone like Henry Ford. The man was a genius. He was really working on a flying toaster when someone said, "Look! It moves on land!" And why would our forebears invent a perfectly good wheel and then surround it with two thousand pounds of breakables?

Every car is a ball and chain. Every child wants one.

It seems just like yesterday I was "driving" my '51 slant-back Chevy the fifty feet from the sidewalk to the end of the driveway and back, over and over and over again. My father well knew the grief ahead yet was powerless to save me. The '51 Chevy was eventually sold to Pinky Timmons for $110, but its evil spawn kept coming:

The four-cylinder ragtop that blew its engine on a mountain pass.

The four-door Cheryll totaled three months before our wedding day—no insurance.

The rear-engine bus with the snapping clutch cables.

The canary-yellow hatchback run over by the city street sweeper.

And my personal favorite, the blue lemon that did not get us to the one-time-only Pacific Northwest performance of the Vienna Boys Choir. We had planned on it for weeks. Sixty dollars worth of non-refundable tickets in hand, children squirming in delighted anticipation, and the car died on the freeway fifty miles short of "Brahm's Lullaby." The rest of the night was spent at the garage explaining why Daddy's face was so flushed.

In all fairness, we did sing Christian praise tunes while waiting for a state trooper. But while the kids preferred "Happiness Is," I'm afraid my tastes ran more towards endless stanzas of "Onward Christian Soldiers" to a kind of grim martial beat.

"'Victory in Jesus!'" the family insisted.

"Melodies for martyrs!" I growled back.

The kids seriously believe we should be a six-car family. If Mom and Dad can each have a car, then it only stands to reason that as each child gains a motor vehicle license, each should gain a car.

I call it bondage. They call it freedom.

It's partly my fault. I gladly took them to the K-Mart parking lot after hours to knock the rough edges off of their driving skills before handing them over to driver's education classes. If it had been up to their mother, they would have been taught by remote control. She says I went too far, allowing them to "thread the needle" between the narrow steel pillars of the revolving neon sign before they even learned to parallel park.

She should talk. I think she was the only one with thirty "kills" at the county fair bumper cars pavilion. My little crash-car cutie!

And doesn't learning to drive come at the worst possible time in a child's life? Here they are trying to get out from under, and require less, parental authority and rule, while at the same time having to abide by a new level of law enforcement authority in their lives with its own complex set of rules and laws.

As drivers, for the first time in their lives they are literally turned loose upon society—a lethal weapon in their hands—and told to be responsible. There's such a stunningly short sixteen years difference between doing the backstroke in mother's womb and driving her to Aunt Clara's for the weekend.

Cars are a mixed blessing, but they make our lives easier and more fun. Teens pick up on that right away. Like cars, life has its frustrations, yet teens are just as eager to get out there in the middle of the excitement of it all. Part of parenting is understanding our need to coach them into maturity, give them driving lessons if you will, in spite of all the dangers and frustrations we see ahead—in spite of our own struggles with those same dangers and frustrations.

> IT TAKES DISCERNMENT—GOBS OF IT—TO SAFELY MAKE THE TRANSITION FROM KID TO ADULT IN EIGHTEEN BRIEF YEARS. AS ONE OF YOUR CHILD'S BEST FRIENDS, STAY BY THEIR SIDE THE WHOLE TIME.

In bringing **them up in the training and instruction of the Lord** (Ephesians 6:4), sometimes I'm in the shadows, sometimes on stage, but always I am there, teaching right from wrong and modeling the discernment it takes to tell the difference. Oh, how vulnerable that makes me and how important. A life on the take, one that constantly seeks personal advantage over others, is much more easily justified when we can no longer distinguish between what is pure and true and that which is evil and false. Fathers and mothers need to stand in the gap for their children and demonstrate a discernment that agonizes over getting it right. This is especially true in a materialistic society where from a distance plastic looks like wood. Buy a fancy plastic planter for your bonsai, and you'll pay fifty dollars. Buy a frozen entree, and they throw in the same "planter" for free. Plus, it's microwaveable.

Helping your kids sort illusion from reality is risky business. Humorist Garrison Keillor tells the story of the dad who took his children to a one-ring circus. The elephant was staked out back, and for a treat Dad drove up beside the hungry pachyderm so the kids could feed it peanuts. Well, once that elephant's long, snuffling, snaky trunk took over the inside of the car, Dad had second thoughts. And when the elephant raised the left side of the car two feet off the ground, lurid headlines flashed across Dad's anxious mind, "Family of Six Crushed by Elephant Due to Father Error."

Father error. What a scary thought. I never want to be wrong because I see myself as Tevye in *Fiddler on the Roof.* I am "the papa, the PAPA!" the biggest, burliest person in this family. It's important for me still to be able to flip my 180-pound son over my back. I don't ever want my children to see me weak. But as Keillor goes on to point out, there is a limit even to paternal competency. And when that competency fails, love covers.

Daughter Steph and I joke about the formless brown shapes that sometimes emerge from the oven when she's in a baking mood. They are quite delicious, but they sometimes fail to come out picture-perfect. We call them her "brownie wads." To look at them is to put a scowl on the face of Betty Crocker. To grin and poke each other over them is to turn a sow's ear into a silk purse. To eat them with milk is to die for.

My camp biscuits are legendary failures, a continual source of merriment, and good for skipping across the lake if they didn't pose a danger to wildlife. On the last camping trip, Shane was invited to cook supper, and his beautiful slabs of expensive, honeyed ham went sliding off the hibachi into a sandy gully. They were dutifully rescued, brushed off, and presto, "Sandy Ham" was added to our imaginary *Cookery for Cuckoo Campers, Volume I.* That's how you fail creatively. Laugh it off, and love it up.

Much is made of excellence in corporate America that flows from the freedom to fail. Employees who are allowed to fail without getting axed are the ones willing to take risks that often pay big corporate dividends, and the ones who give the best customer service because they are not afraid of making judgment calls on the spot. Sure the odd call backfires, but far more succeed and create lots of goodwill. The company benefits from happier customers and happier employees.

If my kids know they can fail without being disowned, they will cut me slack when I fail. They know by now that I too suffer from ring around the collar, my shoes need an occasional polishing, and when I smell my best, it probably came from a bottle of *Wild Country.*

LAUGH AT YOURSELF IN FRONT OF YOUR CHILDREN.

I guess I'm kind of like the sound effects man in the old radio dramas. We've taken the kids to a few tapings of radio mysteries, and they are especially fascinated with the work of a veteran Hollywood behind-the-scenes man. He closes car doors, walks on gravel, answers the doorbell, and sloshes water right on cue for thousands of listening ears. He has made much of his own sound effects equipment and 95 percent of the time is competent, assured, and right on. At the last taping, though, he smashed some dishes in the right spot, but cut himself in the process. The blood was real and it was not in the script. He shrugged it off. Hazard of the job. We admired him nonetheless. In fact, we wanted more of what only he could give.

It's the same with the actors. They occasionally flubbed it, but so accomplished and silver-tongued were they the majority of the time that when they did bungle a line, it made them seem all the more wonderful and human. They were instantly forgiven, the lines retaped, and the end product was a happy celebration of talent and timing.

I am like that for my kids. I am usually comfortable and confident in my dad role, but when I do blow it, I'm able to shrug it off and go on, the temporarily wounded hero. At other times, I'm like the dad with the elephant in the car. I break into a cold sweat and contemplate the dire consequences of my actions upon my family, my friends.

MAKE UP STORIES IN WHICH YOUR CHILD IS THE HERO OR HEROINE.

Once when I was seven years old, a local radio station in Oakland, California, held a treasure hunt. Daily clues pointed listeners to a spot somewhere in the city where a certificate for five thousand dollars was hidden. My mother listened faithfully, and on the day the final clue was given, she knew the treasure could be found in one of the large municipal parks. She, my dad, and I jumped in the car and headed for fame and fortune.

About that time, ten thousand other people jumped in their cars and headed for the same park and, presumably, the same fame and fortune. Everyone staked out a piece of park to comb and when that got old, they switched places and recombed.

Along about midday, Mother, sweaty, irritable, and decidedly fed up with most of humanity (including my father), eyed a prime piece of real estate that didn't look as if it had yet been examined. With good reason. It was a patch about forty feet above on what appeared to be a nearly perpendicular slope. Dad was six feet two and Mom was a lady; therefore, I was elected. I approached from a sidewalk at the top, inching down what I perceived to be the highest cliff in the world, if not North America (my sense of geography was not yet fully developed), until I became thoroughly terrified to go either up or down. I froze.

I also began to wail, which did nothing for Mother's disposition. A crowd formed and their looks said it all. What mother would subject her child to so precarious a place for a measly five thousand dollars? Every mother there, if they'd thought of it first. I wailed all the louder, and Mother made it quite clear to Father that if a hook and ladder truck had to respond, the resulting circus would not be her idea of a fun afternoon. He performed a heroic stretch and snatch, and I was safe at last.

On the way home, empty-handed, I saw tears at the corners of Mother's eyes. I patted her hand, thinking she was disappointed over not finding the treasure. Then she looked at me and said, "Oh, Clinty, I was so afraid you would fall. I'm so glad you weren't hurt." Not until I became a father did I learn that she was also blaming herself for frightening me.

My children, how often I have felt inadequate for you:

For you, Steph, that I was not there the time a man proposi-tioned you, or the time you dislocated your shoulder on the sledding slope, or when you were sick in a tent in the Amazon jungle. I was not there when you stepped off the plane after it had nearly

WHEN

COMPETENCY

FAILS,

LOVE

COVERS.

crashed, but believe me when I say that I wish so deeply that I had been. And I can't wait to meet the cocker spaniel puppy that we were never able to get for you. Maybe you'll name him Giggles after all the good times we've had.

For you, Shane, when you needed a dad who could make things of wood and scrap, who would jog with you in the mornings, and who could show you the inner workings of a car. I never could do those things, but how proud I was the day you came home from your part-time job at the vacuum store, having repaired your very first "frammis." I know you would tell me that I am what I am and that's plenty good enough for you.

GET EXCITED OVER YOUR CHILDREN'S DREAMS. WHEN THEY EXPRESS A DESIRE TO BECOME A TEACHER OR A CHEF, TAKE IT SERIOUSLY AND BRAINSTORM TOGETHER FOR WAYS TO REACH THEIR GOAL.

For you, Amy, when you had that viral infection—your eyes swelled shut, and your body puffed up like a Cabbage Patch Doll's. How we missed the joy in those laughing eyes of yours. To never see them again would have been an enormous loss, for every time they lit upon me, they would ignite with sparks of delight. And what was more amazing than to see you and Mommy exchanging laughing glances over some rich bit of news? When finally those pretty "peepers" emerged from their hiding place of several days, it was as if a prolonged eclipse of the sun had ended at last.

For you, Nate, when you were six weeks old and awoke in the night with labored breathing. You would catch your breath and not breathe again for too long. Mother and I would hold our breath with you, for what good was it for us to breathe when you could not? We walked the floor with you and begged you, "Breathe,

Buddy, that's a good boy. Breathe for Daddy. Breathe for Mommy." The doctor said we should take you for a drive in the cool night air, and we did. Oh, how sweet when at last you looked at me over the back of your mother's shoulder, bright-eyed and wobbly-headed, as if to say, "Gee, Dad, this is neat. Can we go for drives more often?"

Ah, kids, can we ever recapture that day we walked on top of the Red River in a frozen Manitoba winter, and you anxiously asked if it was really safe? You mostly remembered me canoeing on that river, and to walk upon it was still a bit of fairy magic. I shall never forget how you stretched your little legs in order to plant your boots in my wide footprints and how good it was to at last reach shore and thaw our noses together over steamy mugs of Mama's creamy hot chocolate.

I was competent that day. I knew what you did not know and could do what you could not do. I was in every way your father, friend, and protector. You needed me as much as you have ever needed me, and were I to have run away from you then, you would have felt completely and inconsolably abandoned.

You need me so much less now. You have discovered most of my incompetencies and have seen my feet of clay. You have experienced father error and know the whereabouts of most of my warts. And, of course, you love me still.

But none of this has changed your minds about getting a car apiece, has it?

Parents need to be especially careful of teenage tenderness. Kids so quickly forget their victories in a mad rush to broadcast their failings. Parents don't help when they pounce on the failing as if it were indicative of a life of crime. I must be careful of that.

Whenever some weirdness arises in a child of mine, I tend to exaggerate its significance. I'm certain that it does, in fact, indicate there was possibly a mix-up in the maternity ward. For example— the Banana Peel Incident.

My wife pulled up to a stop light as my son was finishing his banana. Instead of depositing the peel into the auto litter basket provided for that purpose, he pitched it into the bed of a pickup truck in the next lane.

He knew it was rude and uncalled for the minute the peel left his hand. Jesus would not have deposited His banana peel in someone else's pickup. The perpetrator's mother got mad at him, I got mad at him, and it was quite clear that he was a turkey. He gave me one of those embarrassed/annoyed looks that said, "I'm not on drugs, I don't sleep around, I've robbed no banks, and I floss every morning. Can we get beyond this?"

We were right, and he was right. It was not something to be proud of, and we should not have laughed it off. We didn't. However, it was not something he was in the habit of doing, and it should be fairly quickly forgotten. It was.

> BELIEVE IN YOUR CHILDREN WHEN THEY ARE SHAKIEST. SAY, "HEY, NOT TO WORRY. EVEN WINSTON CHURCHILL HAD TO REPEAT SIXTH GRADE. LET'S SEE HOW WE CAN GET YOU OVER THE HUMP!"

Create a home environment where there is no freedom to fail, and your child will lose heart. Ignore something very out of character in his behavior, and he will lose respect. It's a balancing act, to be sure, but good friends know it's worth the bother.

Every active writer experiences plenty of rejection. Some see it as failure, others as a stepping stone. While most of the rejection slips in my life have been of the standard photocopied variety, a creative gem slips through now and then that shows a particular sensitivity to this business of success and competency.

A new American humor magazine was about to debut, and they showed an interest in a short story of mine for one of their first issues. Then the funding dried up and they had to inform me that they would have to cease publication. The editor enclosed a crisp one-dollar bill and these words: "We regret not being able to publish you. Please accept this dollar as a token of our esteem."

Probably my all-time favorite is this response from a Christian satire magazine to my idea for a new comic strip:

Dear Clint,

Thank you for sending us your comic strip, "Heaven Help Us." The strip is clever, but it is just not right for *The Wittenburg Door*. I'm sorry, but it may be the best thing that ever happened to your career. A recent Gallup Poll indicated that 95 percent of the cartoonists who had their material published in our magazine are now working at truck stops. The other 5 percent refuse to answer their mail.

Thanks again for thinking of us. Cordially,
Mike Yaconelli,
Keeper of the *Door*

Our families, our friends, count on us to be creative in both our acceptance and correction of their flaws. Cars can be replaced. Families are forever.

Chapter 15

MUSIC, CHURCH, SPORTS, AND FRIED SQUIRREL

Have you ever had fried squirrel? I had one once.

I was in charge of a poultry operation of nearly four thousand broiler chickens. One hot summer day when they were just about ready for market, the electrical power to the barn shut down and 866 prime birds suffocated to death. No electricity meant no exhaust fans. No exhaust fans meant a choking build-up of ammonia from the chicken manure. Cut off from their oxygen supply, the chickens stampeded for the outside walls where air drafts were located. One quarter of the flock died in the panic.

When I discovered the disaster and opened the doors later that day, I was met with a horrible hissing sound. At first I thought it was propane gas escaping, but soon discovered it was the collective sound of chickens gasping for breath. Heartsick, my workers and I removed the carcasses in wheelbarrows and drove them to the dump where a bulldozer covered them with dirt.

The insurance covered floods, hurricanes, and airplanes falling from the sky. What it didn't cover was a squirrel's appetite. A little squirrel had visited the transformer at the top of the power pole servicing the chicken barn. Its light snack of powerline insulation was shockingly brief. The transformer shorted out, and the chickens died before their time.

A two-pound squirrel had annihilated four thousand pounds of chickens.

In the same way, we cannot insulate our children against every possible eventuality. Some things just aren't covered in the policy. There are lots of dumb clucks and squirrels out there who can change our carefully balanced equation in the blink of an eye, but that shouldn't stop us from doing all we can to ensure that our growing kids have plenty of air with which to make clear-headed decisions.

Church, sports, and music provide great quantities of oxygen for the young decision-maker. We've used these same things to hone the Three Senses, but they also have value in training our children to make wise decisions in the face of what life can throw at them. By no means are they co-equal in significance, but we shall treat them as a group because all have played important roles in shaping our children to be our friends and providing ways for them to cope with the ups and downs in their futures.

PRAY ALOUD WITH YOUR CHILD AND GIVE GOD PRAISE FOR "BILLY'S" OR "SARAH'S" BEST QUALITIES.

God wants us to come together to worship Him on a consistent basis, and He promises a long and fulfilled life to those who make a priority of seeking Him first. To deny your children this fundamental prerequisite for a productive existence is to deny them the most important ingredient for a loving, successful life. It is no wonder that families who do not attend church together often drift apart. Why should children honor us, obey us, or find us the least bit interesting if we have kept from them, and ourselves, the standards for right living established by God?

Conversely, parents who make church attendance a thing of mere duty and regimental drudgery will find their children resenting them and God. But corporate worship, youth rallies, and sound, consistent biblical teaching will refine and deepen our children's understanding of spiritual things. So many kids today are a mile wide and an inch deep in their understanding of and commitment to just about anything imaginable. Their lives are full of distractions and busyness, but how much of anything meaningful and life-lasting do they receive? As their parents and good friends, we need to give them spiritually protein-rich meat to eat.

One Saturday, my son and daughter and their mother attended a Christian youth leadership conference. The group is Christian Endeavor, with roots back to the 1800s. My son was state president, and my daughter was in charge of cultivating new churches for membership. They learned to take principal leadership within the church and realized that religious faith is far more than reciting the books of the Bible or learning all the verses to "Amazing Grace," as basic and good as those things may be. They now understand that faith is central to life, that to be a fully functioning human being in this world, an individual needs to have citizenship in the next. It is possible to establish permanent residency in heaven now. The sure knowledge of their right standing in God's sight provides children with enormous confidence, no matter what life throws at them.

Faith teaches them humility, morality, courage, optimism, love, hospitality, charity, fidelity, and selflessness. Faith provides perspective and calm in a world of anxiety. Riots, recession, and radioactivity will not traumatize a child of the King of Glory. Faith refreshes, restores, renews, and rekindles their spirits in difficult times. Racism, hatred, vandalism, and delinquency are not part of such a child's repertoire. And parents, in the eyes of their offspring, are to be loved, respected, and sought after for their wisdom and guidance.

What family would not benefit from being populated with children like that?

This means, of course, that as parents we cannot take a passive approach to church and faith. We cannot wave good-bye to our children at the church door or look at Sunday school as a baby-sitting service. We must model for them the good life of faith and encourage and affirm them at every turn. If we make church life a natural and necessary part of a whole and productive family life, our offspring will follow our example willingly.

We too often torpedo any hope of staying close and essential in our kids' lives by cutting them off from, or leaving to chance, those things that by their very nature are life-giving and family-strengthening.

Music is a great example. It matters not whether we can sing a note. What matters is making a joyful noise and establishing a covering of good music in the home. In my family, our children have come to appreciate a wide variety of musical style and expression. Sure, they prefer their louder, faster, more contemporary forms, but one night they were dazzled by a virtuoso yodeler. On a camping trip, the boys requested Smokey Mountain gospel hymns played on autoharps, banjos, and hammered dulcimers. In choir, they sang classical, folk, jazz, and spirituals. Country/Western puts in an occasional appearance, and they have attended concerts featuring rock, piano, rap, and Rachmaninoff.

I have found that if parents of teens make a federal case of "their music," they will often drive them to it as a form of protest against what is perceived as parental rigidity. It is far better, and far friendlier,

TEACH YOUR

CHILDREN TO

LOOK UP AT THE

CLOUDS. TELL

THEM, "ONE DAY

JESUS WILL COME

RIGHT THROUGH

THERE LOOKING

FOR YOU!"

to expose them deliberately to the reasonable spectrum and show them what great fun and fulfillment can be had in appreciating a good mix. I kid my children about their "high-speed blender" music, and they tease me about my "elevator oldies," but more often we have good discussions about method and meaning in music.

We have talked about pop star Whitney Houston's secular songs and Christian testimony; about Christian singer Amy Grant's crossover into mainstream rock; about Bach's juxtaposition of minor and major notes to evoke hope in the midst of tribulation; about McDonald's hamburger jingles and how they make us hungry. The entire family was especially moved by the musical score from the Broadway production of *Phantom of the Opera*. But ultimately, our children must understand that we were given music and voice with which to praise and worship God. Nature itself makes melody to its Creator:

The meadows are covered with flocks and the valleys are mantled with grain; they shout for joy and sing.
—Psalm 65:13

Let the rivers clap their hands, let the mountains sing together for joy.
—Psalm 98:8

Sing for joy, O heavens, for the LORD has done this; shout aloud, O earth beneath. Burst into song, you mountains, you forests and all your trees, for the LORD has redeemed Jacob, he displays his glory in Israel.
—Isaiah 44:23

Is anyone happy? Let him sing songs of praise.
—James 5:13

A merry and musical heart is a grateful heart. The family, and interfamily friendships, can't help but gain. We have found choirs to be one of the very best ways to excite kids about music. Whether strong soloists or not, they can usually blend with a choir. High school jazz choirs have enjoyed a resurgence of popularity across the country and provide a wonderful means of musical expression and staging.

Start your kids young. Xylophones, triangles, ukuleles, and even kazoos can excite the melodic possibilities. Cheryll bought each of the kids a musical "joymaker" one Christmas both to use and as a reminder of the large part music has played in our lives together. My parents bought me an accordion and two years of lessons. While so many of us accordion players from the fifties and sixties did not keep up with our instruments, I believe the squeeze box played a significant role in placing a song in the heart of an entire generation. No, I do not remember all the verses to "Yokohama Ferry Boat" or "Never on Sunday," but I can still do a mean bellows shake if the party starts to lag.

QUOTE GOETHE TO YOUR CHILD: "WHATEVER YOU CAN DO, OR DREAM YOU CAN, BEGIN IT. BOLDNESS HAS GENIUS, POWER, AND MAGIC IN IT."

(When I was writing the first draft of this book, I had to chase away a kid who was reading over my shoulder. He had formed the words "oom-pa-pa" with his lips and was holding a little cup like an organ grinder monkey. All such detractors will be sorry one day when the accordion is at last crowned king of the reed instruments.)

A word of caution. Like everything else, music can have unexpected side effects. My wife will never forget accompanying Shane and the Northwest Boychoir to the upscale Westin Hotel for a state dinner with the governor of Washington and his honored guest, the governor of a province in China. My wife thought the boys looked perfectly stunning in their matching dark suits. Then, with a gasp of horror, she saw a flash of misplaced white. White socks! One little urchin was wearing white socks in a sea of black.

The urchin was ours.

My wife was not about to suffer international humiliation. She could not stand the thought of Chinese housewives tittering over the silly little American boy who shamed his nation by wearing crew socks at a black tie affair. She would fix it. And sure enough, when the choir rose to sing with the voices of angels, each and every one was crisp and color-coordinated. Had anyone lifted the dress pant legs of the proud fathers in the audience, however, they would have found one man wearing no socks at all.

Like music, sports can have a therapeutic effect on your children's dispositions if you approach it right. Have fun, give it your best, and be a team player—all are excellent interpersonal skills for which the family will be better off. Aggression in the home can be channeled onto the playing field. There it can also be defused, diluted, or dispersed. Under the tutelage of a good coach, much like the shaping skills of a competent and compassionate military drill sergeant, discipline, self-control, and fair play can be earned and enjoyed.

The players will listen to the coach.

Cheryll made it a priority to go the extra mile to support Nate in his love of baseball. All the other kids majored in soccer. Baseball was all Nate's. So Cheryll ran the candy sale, helped administrate the Little League, and operated a tournament concession stand. Nate saw her in action, benefited from her stick-to-it-tiveness and

TAKE OUT AN INEXPENSIVE AD IN THE "SPECIAL OCCASIONS" OR "PERSONALS" SECTION OF THE CLASSIFIEDS: "JERRY SMITH IS THE WORLD'S MOST SPECIAL AND TALENTED KID!"

insights, and worked with her in concession sales. He knew that because baseball was important to him, it was important to us.

In addition to baseball and soccer, our children have all gained from athletic competition including cross-country, fencing, wrestling, basketball, and track. One child went out for pole vaulting and never cleared the bar the entire season. Body type and its limitations became better understood. But no less effort went into the trying, the mental preparation, and the physical conditioning.

Closer to home, we've worked out some of our interpersonal "bugs" with sessions under the barbells, on the tennis court, and out in the yard playing keep away. The kids see their mom and dad head for the volleyball court every Monday night. That's our playtime with the over-thirty-five crowd. We laugh, we joke, we sweat, we fall down. Not a bad recipe for family, actually. Make time with your kids to laugh, joke, sweat, and fall down together. You'll spend less time being at odds with one another.

And never lose sight of Paul's great sports analogies, especially about running the race of this world well to attain the prize of everlasting life in heaven. (See Philippians 3:14; 1 Corinthians 9:24-26; Ephesians 6:12; 2 Timothy 4:8.)

MAKE A VIDEOTAPE OF YOUR CHILDREN'S MUSIC AND SPORTS ACTIVITIES AND LET THEM HELP YOU EDIT IT. SEND COPIES TO SELECTED RELATIVES AND FRIENDS.

There you have it. Sing while you race to church. Exhale, exert, and exalt. Recognize that your whole being and that of each of your children is an instrument meant for praise. Convince them to think of their lives as hymns written by the Master Composer. Their bodies, whether in action, in repose, or in adoration—like the hills and the trees—ought to shout of the existence of God Almighty.

You'll still fight over the car keys, find empty juice pitchers in the fridge, and freeze in the shower because the hot water's all gone. But remember, someday the house will be all yours again, along with all the emptiness. For now, keep 'em close and don't sweat the small stuff. Someday the clatter will only be a memory, and you will remember how it once was music to your ears.

Chapter 16

A FAMILY RESEMBLANCE

Cheryll and I once attended the carnival with my best friend and his wife. Invited to lose my lunch on something called the Zipper, the Dipper, or the Stomach Ripper—I forget which—I declined. But I did agree to the Mad Mouse. This little mechanical torture rack sends you careening down spaghetti-thin rails, making a series of hairpin turns calculated to put a rag doll in traction.

Safely back on solid ground, I allowed my wife to lead me by the hand until heaven and earth resumed their rightful places. She guided me into a sideshow tent featuring the incredible Gorilla Lady. Right before our very eyes, a lovely damsel would be transformed into a ferocious ape creature. Still wondering if I would ever again eat a double corn dog with extra mustard and a cotton candy appetizer, I bravely pressed forward into the tent.

We were among the last to be admitted and were far from the front of the stage. On top of that, everyone ahead of us seemed like six-foot-six giants. My five-foot-one little darling couldn't see to blow her nose, let alone the wonders about to unfold somewhere up ahead.

Suddenly, the house lights dimmed, the stage lights brightened, the damsel appeared, and the transformation began. Slowly, subtly, the woman's features began to blur and thanks to the guy in the projection booth, she gradually got furry around the edges. Thanks further to strobe lighting and the switching off of every brain in the place, the woman "faded" clean away and a guy in a hairy gorilla suit charged the audience with a mild roar. We responded with a weak collective scream and "fled" the tent for our very lives.

Back outside, I struggled to keep my corn dogs from revolting, and my wife asked, "What, where, what happened? I couldn't see a thing. Why were people screaming? Why'd we run away?"

Why had we paid $1.75 a ticket?

"You mean to tell me you didn't see a thing that happened in there?" I huffed, searching about desperately for a place to lie down. Why don't carnivals supply emergency cots for Mad Mouse victims?

"See?" she seethed. "I was lucky to be able to breathe!"

I knew exactly what she meant. I was having a little trouble breathing myself.

We've relived the memory many times since, and I tell her it was no big deal; she will always be the "girl-illa" in my dreams. She laughs and pokes me in the ribs, and I remind her that it didn't take a rocket scientist to see the sham that she had so mercifully been spared.

In the make-believe hokum of the carnival world, there was no resemblance between the attractive woman and the gorilla she "became." In the real course of our daily lives, however, there is wonderful connectedness. Our children bear our physical likeness, just as we reflect the physical likeness of our parents. And how often do we hear comments from others like the following?

CARRY A PICTURE OF YOUR CHILDREN ON YOUR KEY CHAIN.

"She sings as beautifully as her sister. The resemblance is uncanny!"

"He has his dad's best features, don't you think?"

"I can't get over how much those two look alike!"

"Two peas in a pod, that's what they are!"

How often we see signs of a person's finer qualities in another relative. Joyous are those occasions when the best in Uncle Joe surfaces in a nephew, or when the easy laughter and sensitivity of a mother comes to full bloom in her daughter. We cherish the similarities and celebrate the continuation in another generation of the qualities we love in someone near and dear to us. Usually the persons to whom we pay these compliments are flattered and genuinely pleased at the comparison. We've praised the family traits about them that we enjoy the most, and they rightly bask in the family honor.

But there is a higher compliment to be paid in the family of God, and we ought to look for occasions in which to bestow it. Once, while thinking of the ultimate compliment to pay my wife for the Christlike qualities of compassion, generosity, and selflessness she so often lives, I thought back to those family gatherings and the heartfelt compliments that flowed. I looked at her and knew exactly what to say: "I see so much of the Lord in you!"

TELL YOUR CHILD THAT HE OR SHE IS A MIGHTY MAN OR WOMAN OF GOD JUST LIKE THE ONES IN THE BIBLE. EXPLAIN WHAT GOD CAN DO WITH SOMEONE WHO LOVES HIM WITH ALL THEIR HEART.

We are created in God's image and ought at all times to strive to be more like Him. That is the pattern for life that we must model for our children if we want to remain close friends. The family resemblance within the Kelly household, not only in the physical, but more importantly in attributes, attitudes, and actions, should present a slice of what it's like to be a part of the family of God. Your children will thank you and have so much in common with you if these are the things you focus on in their upbringing.

Scripture is replete with compliments for those actively seeking a heavenly family resemblance. In Hebrews 11, commendations are handed down to a number of Old Testament faithfuls. Verse 38 tells us **the world was not worthy of them** because they displayed such godly qualities with such far-reaching results.

What amazing regard God had for Mary that she should be found worthy to bear the Messiah!

I consider the Roman centurion whose humility, compassion, and faith in Jesus' healing power astonished the Lord and resulted in His commendation, **I have not found anyone in Israel with such great faith** (Matthew 8:10).

Who among God's servants does not crave to one day at the throne of grace hear those words of holy praise for fidelity and service, "Well done, good and faithful servant"? With that in mind, we should embark on a voyage of discovery. We are in search of the divine qualities in our children.

Steph spent her free time with the homeless and those in prison. Good for you, honey; that's where Jesus spent so much of His time.

Shane loved to dig in the garden and sing God's praise. Way to go, son; honest working hands and a worshipful heart please God.

Amy served others without pay and cultivated a sweet, gracious spirit. Bless you, darlin'; for the merciful will be shown mercy.

Nate sweated at being a top student and much of the time was my jolly Sir Laugh-A-Lot. Nice work, buddy; the joy of the Lord will be your strength.

Everywhere in my past I can find examples of those who modeled true friendship and a Christlike attitude. They need to hear what a difference they made in my life and how important the way they treated me has been in my being able to form lasting friendships with my children.

Thank you, Harry Ketrenos, my best friend and college buddy. You were there when my mom and dad died, and you let me lean hard on your good nature throughout the foolishness of youth. Thank you, Brian Powell, a friend of unflagging cheerfulness, willing even to fund my writing efforts and not count the cost. Thank you, Caroline and Charlie Belton, for loving us and our children whether we were near or far from you, and asking nothing in return.

And thank you, Cheryll Kelly, my gift from God and closest friend until death do us part. Without your tender, forgiving ways and generous laughter, I would be so much the poorer.

But now I need to take my search into the church where my children should witness my example of looking for the heavenly family resemblance. I see it in the friendly greeters who melt the world's ice and tenderize my heart with their smiles. I see it in my busy pastor who nevertheless met individually with the mayor, the police chief, the newspaper editor, and the school superintendent to tell them how important they are to the community and to let them know that ours is a caring and praying church that takes its role in town seriously. He has invited some of them to speak at the church and has been appointed to a ministerial advisory committee to the school district.

I see it in the teenager who, for a Sunday school class on religious oppression in the world, "smuggled" her Bible into class by braiding it into her hair. I see it in the preteen who tithes on her paper route

TELL YOUR CHILD

WHAT A GOOD

FRIEND THEY ARE.

"I CAN ALWAYS

COUNT

ON YOU!"

money, and in the boy who gives up a Saturday evening to help a local ministry move offices.

One Sunday morning at church, I was blue. My wife was home with a cold and, despite the exuberance of the four Kelly kids, the empty space at my side was unfillable.

Then I glanced at the senior couple in the pew ahead. They were holding hands and basking in one another's love and God's blessing. Without their knowing it I borrowed a little of their love, for it was not for themselves alone. Because they were so satisfyingly one in the holy bond, we all gained.

The next day I was prompted to write a note of thanks to that couple and tell them what a genuine comfort they had been to the Gloomy Gus behind them. At first, I balked. Surely it would embarrass them that someone had taken particular note of their handholding in church. On the contrary. They needed to know that their affectionate display of God's love in their lives did not go unnoticed.

I wrote the note and the following Sunday I was hugged mightily by the missus to whom it had been in part addressed. I came to find out the couple had been quarreling some, and my compliment about what their affection for one another had meant to me had in turn made them realize what was truly important in their own lives. Double blessings like these are God's specialty.

On another Sunday, I noticed the rare absence of an older member and called her at home to tell her I'd missed her. There was a short pause before she said softly, "I didn't even think anyone noticed I was there."

How she needed to hear that she mattered, that as old as she was, she was not without influence. Her steadfast anchor in the solid rock of Jesus was a help to less mature Christians.

Confirmation and approval in the Lord's work are among the wisest investments of human praise. So why do I do it so infrequently? I shouldn't wait for the heavenly family reunion every Sunday to express a compliment. I need to pray for the wisdom to recognize heavenly family traits at anytime in anyone and to open my mouth and eagerly pay the compliment without delay.

Another favor I can do for my kids is to point them to creative examples of faith in action outside of church. Ron Jones is one example. He is a music composer for television and film, one of the tops in the business. Perhaps he is best known for his creative musical scores for television's popular *Star Trek: The Next Generation.* His clients read like a Who's Who of Hollywood and include MGM, Columbia, Paramount, Warner Brothers, and Orion. Disney hired him to score the cartoon series, *Duck Tales.* By the age of thirty, he had probably created more musical scores for the entertainment industry than most contemporary composers twice his age.

But first and foremost, Ron is a Christian. "Hollywood's been a harder route for me than going into contemporary Christian music," he says. "I have a testimony to the people I work with . . . I'm carrying a light. Near as I can tell, I'm one of the few."

His harshest critics are in the church. They believe he is engaged in a sinful industry with no redeeming value. But when he is in a room with a giant orchestra and the pressure is on, he asks God to help him make a positive difference in the outcome of a film. He knows God is his ultimate judge.

Ron graduated from the Christian institution where I work, Seattle Pacific University. He was challenged for greatness there by the heavenly family resemblance and creative genius of authors like C. S. Lewis and J. R. R. Tolkien. He was told by the university president that the world is in desperate need of Christian shoe salesmen who are the very best shoe salesmen they can be.

Armed with the Word of God and the tools of computers and music synthesizers, he believes he can actually turn a negative film project around, emphasizing the good and empathizing with the positive. He gives the example of an original version of a film that glorifies the villain. In the final cut, it may be possible to throw audience support behind the victims because of the emotional persuasion evinced by Jones' music. He believes that if Christians are clear on their ideas and innovative in their approach, a renaissance of spiritual creativity can affect society.

Our children, especially, need to hear that. They can model virtue anywhere in the world if God calls them there. Let us commend them every time they take a stand and reject greedy and often lascivious role models in favor of Noah, Moses, Ruth, Esther, Saint Paul, Mother Teresa, and Ron Jones. Our kids deserve our applause when they are righteously discriminating. Does not the heavenly host break into a noisy cheer over one repentant sinner? Let's throw a party for our kids when they choose the salvation and wisdom of God over the sin and shame of this world. For them to hear, "I see so much of the Lord in you," is to have planted in them the seeds of desire for the sterling characteristics so perfectly blended in Jesus Christ.

TELL YOUR CHILDREN HOW MUCH YOU ADMIRE THEM WHEN THEY DO OR SAY SOMETHING REMARKABLE.

To call our children mighty men and women of God is to tell them that they can walk with God. To name them "warriors of the Cross," "servants of the King," "inheritors of the kingdom of heaven," or other biblical titles is to provide them with lofty standards to which to attain. How they, and we as their family and friends, must stretch in a commitment to God and His principles to rightfully bear those titles!

Do you remember the first part of the Kelly family vision statement? "We have been given to each other in order to spur one another on to personal excellence." It takes work for people to be one in unity of purpose and vision, whether they comprise an office, a congregation, or a family of six. It takes a great deal of humility and effort to become unconsumed with ourselves and devoted to the growth of the other person. Philippians 2 gives the perfect example of perfect humility in Christ's stooping to become a man and die on a cross. As my practical pastor puts it, "Philippians 2 shows quite clearly that for true humility to operate, someone must eat dirt."

Pride, arrogance, self-centeredness, and scorn for one another are destroying families left and right. No kid in his right mind wants to be friends with a parent who models those negative traits. No parent can form an easy companionship with a child who is willful and manipulative.

So take the time, whatever else may have to slide, to cultivate your children's sense of purpose, sense of adventure, and sense of humor. Though the dust may be five feet high and rising in our house and no two pieces of furniture match, we have loved our kids with a fierce love, and they have found the true measure of their worth in the very home in which they were raised.

For whatever divine purpose, God gave those particular kids to us. What we do with them, how we make or break them, will affect generations to come. Had we ignored them, overindulged them, or made good on our promise to sell them to the gypsies, we would have missed out on one of the treasures of life.

But what about the scar tissue of parenting? Show it off. It is a mark of honor. Haul out those baby books and remind yourself of the potential in every wiggly one of your children. Here's Cheryll's entry for Nathan at five months: "Nate can roll over on his tummy now, but he can't roll back. So he gets stuck. Then he pounds his little nose in the floor like a woodpecker. He gets so upset!"

Three-year-old Amy got in the habit of flipping Nate over again on his back with a hearty cry of, "Roll the baby!"

Nate's stopped hammering his nose into the floor. Instead, he beats me at rummy, plays a mean third base, laughs when I call him Snotty Paste, and believes in life eternal. He leads a junior high youth group and is engaged to be married. The world would be so much less without him.

So again, I wish you *barrambarri*. May God bless you and bear you up as you travel, mend fences, build bridges, and drain swamps with your kids. To gain their friendship, as well as their confidence and obedience, is well worth the struggle. Don't ever think it's too late to start. Go to them. Make your peace. Tell them that apart from God, there is nothing more necessary in your life than their friendship—not your career, your investments, your possessions, your committee assignments, your golfing buddies, or your pride.

Our children are all twenty-somethings now, but the eighteen years we had each of them in the home were astonishingly rich. No, Nate, you cannot knock out the wall between your room and your sister's. She may want to come home. Shane, thanks for letting me wear your shoes and borrow your tie. Steph, sweetums, couldn't I please convince you that the basic daily adult nutrition requirement is not simply a hamburger a day? And weren't there any safer extracurricular activities to pick than rock climbing? Yes, Amy, if you write down a list of the clothes you need to borrow or want returned, I will see that Steph gets it once a week. No, I don't mind bringing home twice the laundry this year. Honest, I don't.

Hey, anyone want to go camping? You remember that nice little spot on French Shriek? I'm sure that with just a little bushwhacking, we could find it again. And anyone up for TPing this Friday night after the game? We've got a whole case of toilet paper in the basement, and I don't mind driving!

ABOUT THE AUTHOR

Clint Kelly is a communications specialist for Seattle Pacific University, a freelance writer of more than six hundred articles, and a novelist with five published adventures. His articles for kids have appeared in *Breakaway*, *Cobblestone*, and *Child Life* magazines, and for adults in *Charisma*, *Family Circle*, and *HomeLife*. He is presently at work on a true historical adventure.

Clint conducts writers' workshops, hikes in search of sasquatch, and takes an occasional turn at the wok. He has four grown children and has been married to his lovely bride, Cheryll, for twenty-nine years. They make their home in Everett, Washington.

To contact the author, write:

Clint Kelly

504 - 51 Street SW

Everett, Washington 98203

OTHER BOOKS FROM ALBURY PUBLISHING

God's Answers for Your Every Question for Fathers
by Albury Publishing

God's Answers for Your Every Question for Mothers
by Albury Publishing

Jesus Freaks
by dcTalk and The Voice of the Martyrs

Mature Christians Are Boring and Other Myths
About Maturity in Christ
by Ron Luce

Spiritual Shock Treatment
by Ron Luce

Ten Words That Will Change a Nation—The Ten Commandments
by Rob Schenk

Turning the Hearts of the Fathers
compiled by Ron Luce

You Wanna' Pierce What?
by Walker Moore

Additional copies of this book and other book titles
from **ALBURY PUBLISHING** are
available at your local bookstore.

ALBURY PUBLISHING
P. O. Box 470406
Tulsa, Oklahoma 74147-0406

For a complete list of our titles,
visit us at our web site:
www.alburypublishing.com

For international and Canadian orders,
please contact:

Access Sales International
2448 East 81st Street
Suite 4900
Tulsa, Oklahoma 74137
Phone 918-523-5590   Fax 918-496-2822